HELEN

Stairway to the Upper Room

Stairway to the Upper Room

Daily meditation on the
Gospel Readings for Sundays
and Solemnities

Volume I

Ronald Walls

GRACEWING

First published in 2002

Gracewing
2 Southern Avenue, Leominster
Herefordshire HR6 0QF

ISBN 0 85244 565 2

Typeset by Action Publishing Technology Ltd,
Gloucester GL1 5SR

Printed by MPG Books Ltd,
Bodmin PL31 1EG

Contents

PREFACE

Not for the first time, the indefatigable Fr Ronald Walls has done us all a service.

There is no shortage, happily, of commentaries on the Mass readings provided by the Lectionary. But this volume, as its catching title indicates, has its own distinctive approach. It stands out in two ways. First of all, here are no dry as dust exegetical notes on the inspired texts, nor, on the other hand, mere pious ramblings which have little to do with what the Bible is actually saying. Rather, Fr Walls' reflections on the readings deftly insert the passages of a particular Sunday or Solemnity into the full sweep, the whole course, of biblical revelation as understood, transmitted and celebrated by the Church in her eucharistic liturgy. This is in accord with the big-hearted, truly 'catholic' approach to Scripture urged by Vatican II's *Dei Verbum*, and answers the cry of so many listening hearts. Secondly, these volumes provide a guide to meditation and prayer. In this, they reconnect with the ancient link, cherished by the Fathers of the Church and monks, between reading (*lectio*) and prayer (*oratio*). Thus prayer, our poor word to God, is rooted where it should be rooted, in God's word to us, and can take on a new truthfulness. And it is rooted, not in our own sometimes too subjective picking and choosing, but in the Church's calm, liturgical breaking of the bread of the Word, Sunday after Sunday. Once again, Fr Walls has refused to separate what belongs as a whole, and so helps us towards a richer, more integrated Christian life.

May this work lead us up the stairway of Scripture into the presence of the Lord!

Dom Hugh Gilbert, O.S.B.
Abbot of Pluscarden

INTRODUCTION

This book is published in two volumes. The first is devoted to the Scripture readings in the Sunday liturgy which present Salvation History, the tale of the wonderful deeds of God, through which the salvation of mankind has been accomplished. That tale is told partly in the readings from Advent to the conclusion of the Christmas season on the feast of the Baptism of our Lord, and partly in the readings from Lent to the end of the Easter season at Pentecost, to which the feast of the Blessed Trinity and the feast of Corpus Christi are appended. Between the Christmas season and Lent there is a variable number of Sundays in Ordinary Time, and so Volume I includes Sundays 2–12 cycles A, B, and C in Ordinary Time.

Volume II is devoted to the readings for the Sundays 13–34 in Ordinary Time for all three years. The 'ordinary' weeks of the liturgical year are the time when the Christian's attention is directed to the task of perfecting discipleship, of growing in sanctity. Volumes I and II of this book together provide a guide to daily meditation for every week in the three years of the liturgical cycle. Before beginning to follow out the programme of meditation suggested by this book, it may be helpful to consider for a moment what is distinctive about Christian prayer, in particular about Christian meditation.

Prayer

The moment we set foot upon the first step of the stairway of prayer, the urge is born in us to climb up until we find rest in the Upper Room of God's presence. We share the feelings of the psalmist who sang: 'As a doe longs for running streams, so longs my soul for you, my God' (Psalm 42.1). And we are encouraged by the grace of God to believe that this desire will in the end be satisfied. 'What we are to be in the future has not yet been revealed; ... when it is revealed we shall be like him because we shall see him as he really is' (1 John 3.2).

But the Christian who longs for this consummation must be patient; the mere longing to see the face of God does not all at once and without more ado introduce the worshipper into the immediate presence of God. If the initial 'cry of recognition and of love', as St Thérèse of Lisieux called it, is to lead on to union with God, the cry of recognition and love must come to terms with the recognition that we have fallen out with God. St Peter became painfully aware of this when our Lord enabled him to haul in a great catch of fish in the Sea of Galilee. Falling down at Jesus' feet he cried out: 'Leave me, Lord; I am a sinful man' (Luke 5.11).

Men and women cannot by their own moral strength reinstate themselves as friends of God and climb back into paradise. Their only hope is that God come down to them. This hope has been fulfilled. In the Person of his eternal Son, God has come down to earth and reconciled us to himself; and so, at the heart of the Christian Faith stands the affirmation: 'The Word was made flesh, he lived among us, and we saw his glory, the glory that is his as the only Son of the Father, full of grace and truth. From his fulness we have, all of us, received' (John 1.14, 16). On the eve of the Reformation in Scotland, the poet William Dunbar applauded this act of divine condescension in an *Ode On The Nativity*.

Sinners be glad and penance do,
And thank your Maker heartfully;
For he that ye might not come to,
To you is comen full humbly,
Your soules with his blood to buy,
And loose you from the fiend's arrest,
And only of his own mercy;
Pro nobis puer natus est.

The incarnation of the Son of God is the foundation upon which mankind's redemption rests, and is the reality that makes prayer possible. In prayer we want to turn our minds to God, but how do we do this, upon what do we fix our imagination? In St John's Gospel we read: 'No one has ever seen God; it is the only Son, who is nearest the Father's heart, who has made him known' (John 1.18). And so we fix our imaginations and our minds upon the sacred humanity of our Lord, Jesus Christ.

Christian meditation
Meditation for the Christian is that form of prayer which consists mainly in concentrating attention upon the Person of Jesus Christ, upon his actions and his words, for just as it was through his flesh and blood that he redeemed us, transforming us into his own kith and kin, so it is through his sacred humanity that he teaches us and leads us on through prayer towards perfect union with God the Father. To express this thought St Catherine of Siena used a simple and vivid metaphor. God speaks to her:

My sublimity stooped to the earth of your humanity and together they made a bridge and remade the road. And why? So that you might indeed come to the joy of the angels. But it would be no use my Son's having become your bridge to life if you do not use it. (*Dialogue* XXII).

St Teresa of Avila teaches exactly the same truth, stressing that our Lord's sacred humanity is the only means by which we can reach the heights of contemplation. This is what she wrote to Fr Garcia de Toledo:

> It is God's will if we are to please him and he is to grant us great favours, that this should be done through his most sacred humanity, in whom, his Majesty said, he is well pleased. I have seen clearly that this is the door that we must enter if we wish his sovereign Majesty to show us great secrets. Therefore, Sir, even if you reach the summit of contemplation your reverence must seek no other way: that way alone is safe. (*Life* XXII).

Catherine and Teresa were two great Christian mystics, women who through prayer found a very high degree of union with God, and their method was to apply their minds and imaginations to the Person of the incarnate Son of God. Their type of mysticism and of prayer stands in sharp contrast to all other forms of mysticism and the methods of meditation associated with them.

For the nature mystic, union with the deity is achieved by a natural progress, because the substance of the human spirit is regarded as of a piece with the divine Spirit; in its union with God the human soul simply realizes all its natural potential. The beatific vision, on this view, consists in reaching a certain psychic state, progress towards which can be advanced by natural means, such as ascetical practices, hypnotic chanting, even by the use of hallucinatory drugs. For the Christian mystic, on the other hand, God always transcends human nature, and although the end of mankind's redemption is union with God, that union, on the Christian view, is not a merging of like substances but a loving union between persons who remain distinct. The meditation through which the Christian hopes to come ever nearer to union with God makes no attempt to alter the psychic state of the worshipper. All effort in Christian meditation is devoted to coming to know the Christ portrayed in the Gospels, and to listening to him.

It is true that the Christian should pray constantly, for prayer, as St John of Damascus said in the eighth century, is the 'raising of the mind and heart to God'; but there are times when it is appropriate, and indeed necessary for spiritual progress, to set aside times for meditation, times when one makes a conscious effort to get to know our Lord and his teaching better. These are times when it is wise to follow our Lord's advice: 'When you pray, go to your private room and, when you have shut the door, pray to your Father who is in that secret place ...' (Matthew 6.6). The words with which in the eleventh century St Anselm of Canterbury opened his classic work, *Proslogion*, remind us that there is an important place in the Christian's life for the prayer that requires temporary withdrawal from the hurly-burly of life:

> Come now, insignificant man, leave behind for a time your preoccupations; seclude yourself for a while from your disquieting thoughts. Turn aside now from heavy cares and disregard your wearisome tasks. Attend for a while to God and rest for a time in him.

This book is designed to help us meditate systematically and with perseverance upon the Lord who is presented to us in the Scriptures. We will discover, however, that meditation, important as it is, is not the end, but a step in progress towards the consummation of prayer, a consummation that comes not through our effort but from God's gift.

The structure of this book
Because the subject of meditation is the Person and teaching of our Lord Jesus Christ, the most important item for each day's meditation is therefore the Gospel passage, which is indicated but not printed out. In every case it is the Gospel reading for a Sunday or Solemnity, and

appended to this is a short Gospel commentary. This is not an exhaustive exposition of the reading, but merely a stimulus to the intellect and imagination, for meditation ought to be one's own work. Provided also is a short text from the Old Testament which throws light on the main theme of the meditation. This too is often taken from the Sunday liturgical reading, as is the vocal prayer in the form of an excerpt from a psalm. Daily meditation during the week is treated as a continuation of the worship that took place on Sunday.

A method for meditation
Meditation is not the activity of disembodied spirits but of men and women who are flesh and blood, and so like all human activity is learned and can be improved by good technique. At first, learning a technique, going through a sequence of moves, may seem somewhat artificial, but it enables a person to act habitually with ease and efficiency. Each one must pray the prayer that he can pray, but as a rule meditation progresses through a series of phases.

1. Having resolved to meditate daily, one should decide prudently when and for how long one will meditate. Most busy people find that fifteen minutes is a sensible length of time to spend in daily meditation. At what time of day this can best be done depends upon particular circumstances. Having made a decision, however, one should abide by it. People sometimes experience emptiness of mind and dryness of spirit after completing a period of meditation, and become discouraged. Although we may think that nothing has happened during our meditation the Lord will reward in some manner our sacrifice of time. We say that time is money: no one likes to waste time, and so making a sacrifice of a little time-span to be offered to God alone is in itself a declaration that no one is more important than God; it is an act of faith, which is what the Lord desires most of all to find in us. At the end of a day when we may have felt that our meditative prayer never got off the ground, we may well discover that the

whole day has been blessed with amazing tranquillity and a sense of accomplishment.

2. Read the Gospel passage carefully. This may be done at leisure on Sunday at the beginning of the week or on the evening before the meditation is to be made. It is useful to have the Gospel passage at hand whilst one is meditating, so that memory can be refreshed if need be.

3. Make a brief examination of conscience. This is essential because prayer cannot be severed from life, and nothing so much impedes prayer as a disorderly life. This *examen* is better done on the evening before the meditation, and it should not be prolonged. It is counter-productive to become too introspective during meditation. St Teresa of Avila gives wise counsel on this subject.

> There is no state of prayer, however sublime, in which it is not necessary to go back to the beginning. And self-knowledge with regard to sin is the bread which must be eaten with food of every kind, however dainty it may be, on this road.

Then she warns against the temptation to wallow in self-analysis.

> But bread must be taken in moderate proportions. It will be wiser to go on to other matters which the Lord sets before us, and we are not doing right if we neglect such things, for his Majesty knows better than we what kind of food is good for us. (*Life* XIII).

4. Immediately before beginning the meditation proper, two preliminary petitions ought to be made. The first is for the gift of total detachment from every worldly interest or care; the second is for grace to understand whatever is presented in the Gospel text, so that it may transfigure our lives. These petitions may be expressed in one's own words. Here are two models.

a. Almighty Father, give me grace to desire only to serve and praise your divine Majesty; free my mind from every concern, and lead my thoughts to your incarnate Son, so that I may return to you, our Father in heaven, and in you find peace.

b. By the light of your Holy Spirit, Lord, enable me to understand what I have read in the Gospel, and to be transfigured in accord with what I have learned. I ask this through Jesus Christ our Lord.

5. When the curtain rises as a play begins, we focus our eyes on the set and on the characters who are about to live out the drama. So it is with Scripture-based meditation. In imagination we see the physical setting in which characters begin to act and to speak.

Ignatius of Loyola recommends that meditation can best begin by our attending carefully to the details of the physical setting. This will anchor our mind and imagination. Following this we should listen carefully to the words of our Lord, and also to what the other characters say. Likewise we take note of all that is done by the characters and all that happens to them.

6. Next we try to understand our Lord's teaching and the meaning of the action. This part of the meditation may prompt us to study the Faith more diligently, but such activity cannot adequately be carried out in fifteen minutes' meditation, and in any case we ought not to prolong this phase of meditation indefinitely, for there is more to meditation than seeking to understand.

7. From this phase of meditation, wherein the imagination and intellect are active, we move more deeply into the Gospel scene, seeking now to stand on the stage with our Lord, to be in his presence and to speak quite naturally with him, as one speaks to a friend.

St Teresa of Avila describes how, long before she became a nun, she used to meditate:

My method of prayer was this. As I could not reason

with my mind, I would try to make pictures of Christ inwardly; and I used to think I felt better when I dwelt on those parts of his life when he was most often alone. It seemed to me that his being alone and afflicted, like a person in need, made it possible for me to approach him. I had many simple thoughts of this kind. I was particularly attached to the prayer in the Garden, where I would go to keep him company. I would think of the sweat and of the affliction he endured there. I wished I could have wiped that grievous sweat from his face, but I remember that I never dared to resolve to do so, for the gravity of my sins stood in the way. I used to remain with him there for as long as my thoughts permitted it. (*Life* IX).

If we persevere in this sort of meditation, after a time we shall become aware that we are rising higher and higher up the stairway of prayer until finally we arrive at the door of the Upper Room.

Contemplation
Behind that door is the Holy of Holies, the sanctuary of God's presence, and once in that room we have entered the contemplative phase of prayer; but we cannot force entrance, we must knock and wait until the Lord opens the door for us, and walks with us into the room, just as he walked with the Twelve into the Upper Room to institute the Holy Eucharist. In that room through the sacrament of his Body and Blood he enabled them to enjoy, as never before, communion with God the Father.

We must bear in mind that our Lord's purpose was to open up for us the way to the Father – 'No one can come to the Father except through me' (John 14.6); but when he has opened the door of the Holy of Holies for us he steps aside. At the Last Supper he affirmed: 'When that day comes you will ask in my name; and I do not say that I shall pray to the Father for you, because the Father himself loves you for loving me and believing that I came from God' (John 16.26–7).

Having accompanied us up the stairway and ushered us into the Father's presence, our Lord's work is complete; his function as Mediator between the Father and mankind has been accomplished; he no longer stands between us and the Father but beside us, leading us in adoration of his Father who is also our Father. Members of his Body, living by his Spirit, sharing in the life of the Blessed Trinity, we are caught up in contemplation of the divine Majesty. In this ultimate phase of prayer, imagery and intellectual activity are left behind; relaxed and in silence, our minds and wills become aligned with the mind and will of God the Father, who blesses us with peace and the assurance of seeing him as he really is in the kingdom of heaven.

At the end of our times of active meditation we leave space for this element of passive contemplation; then we round off our meditation with

Our Father . . . .

The Meditations

THE MEDITATIONS

Advent 1

Old Testament thought:
Oh, that you would tear the heavens open and come
    down
– at your Presence the mountains would melt.

(Isaiah 63.19)

Vocal prayer:
    God of hosts, bring us back;
    let your face shine on us and we shall be saved.
O shepherd of Israel, hear us,
shine forth from your cherubim throne.
O Lord, rouse up your might,
O Lord, come to our help.
God of hosts, turn again, we implore,
look down from heaven and see.
Visit this vine and protect it,
the vine your right hand has planted.
    God of hosts, bring us back;
    let your face shine on us and we shall be saved.

(From Psalm 80)

Gospel: Year A: Matthew 24.37–44; *Year B:* Mark 13.33–7;
Year C: Luke 21.25–8; 34–6

ABC. In the season of Advent we look forward to cele-
brating the birth of our Lord Jesus in Bethlehem; but we
set the Nativity scene against the background of his
Second Coming in glory to judge all mankind. All three
Gospel texts for the first Sunday in Advent contain the
admonition: 'Stay awake!' Our Lord calls us, as we
prepare to rejoice at his birth, to purify ourselves of all sin
and self-seeking, so that we may stand with confidence
before him on the day when he comes as our judge; and
because the hour of his coming is unknown, we must
stand ready in every moment of our lives. Advent is thus
a time for examination of conscience and amendment of
life.

The introduction just before Christmas of the image of
Christ the glorious judge does not diminish the wonder of
the Nativity or our joy on beholding the Child in the
manger. On the contrary, it ensures that we understand
who this Child is. He is not just a sweet infant, but the
'pure emanation of the glory of the Almighty' (Wisdom
7.25). Moreover his birth in the stable-cave at Bethlehem
is also a coming in judgement, for just as his condemna-
tion by Pilate recoiled upon Pilate, so his abasement by
the circumstances of his birth recoils upon the world that
pushed him almost out of sight at his birth.

Conversely, the Nativity enables us to see the Day of
Judgement in true perspective. Our Judge is indeed the
almighty Son of the Most High, but he is also the Son of
Man, who became true man so that, without condoning
any sin, he is full of sympathy with us in our weakness;
and he proved by his passion and death his desire to be
united with us for all eternity. Our Judge is not remote:
he will be judging his own Body, the Church. St Paul
wrote: 'God, by calling you has joined you to his Son,
Jesus Christ; and God is faithful' (1 Corinthians 1.9).
Jesus has told us 'to stand with confidence before the Son

of Man.' Our confidence is not in ourselves, but in God's faithful love. The Church is the Bride of Christ, and so our Lord, our Judge, is as close to us as a man is to his wife. This relationship can be broken only by our refusal to repent of our sins.

Advent 2

Old Testament thought:
His word is a rod that strikes the ruthless,
his sentences bring death to the wicked.   (Isaiah 11.4)

Vocal prayer:
   Come let us return to the Lord.
He has torn us to pieces, but, but he will heal us;
He has struck us down, but he will bandage our wounds;
after a day or two he will bring us back to life,
on the third day he will raise us
and we shall live in his presence.
   Come let us return to the Lord.

(From Hosea 6.1–3)

Gospel: Year A: Matthew 3.1–12; *Year B:* Mark 1.1–8; *Year C:* Luke 3.1–6

ABC. All three evangelists tell of John's call to repentance and his ministry of baptizing in the Jordan river. According to Mark the gospel story begins with the preaching of John the Baptist who, quoting Isaiah, alludes to the whole prophetic tradition, in particular to Elijah who, according to Malachi, was to return to prepare the way for the Messiah. John even assumed Elijah's dress and ate the same food of the wilderness, signs that he was to be identified with this expected forerunner.

The accent on the wilderness, and the fact that 'all the people made their way to him' indicate that God was about to renew his covenant with Israel. John then called the whole people to repentance. The Greek word used means 'a coming to one's senses resulting in a change of conduct'. John proclaimed the imminence of the epoch of the new covenant, that would be ushered in by the One whose baptism would bring not just forgiveness of sins, but the new life of the Holy Spirit.

John stressed that the baptism of the Messiah would be immeasurably greater than the baptism he, John, was able to offer. The baptism of Jesus the Messiah would be no mere legal contract between God and mankind – an amnesty to the sinner – but the inestimable gift of sanctification, a real sharing in the divine life. Such a gift no prophet could ever give; it required the intervention of God himself. From the beginning Mark's Gospel makes clear that Jesus is no less than the Son of God, who has come to confer this very gift.

Despite the incomparable superiority of the dispensation that Jesus was about to inaugurate over the best that John could accomplish, none the less the repentance demanded by John was and still is a necessary precondition of receiving the gift of new life through our Lord Jesus Christ. Advent is a most suitable time for us to note this fact, and to approach the Jordan river, which in our case is the sacrament of penance.

Advent 3

Old Testament thought:
The Lord, the king of Israel, is in your midst;
you have no more evil to fear.   (Zephaniah 3.15)

Vocal prayer:
Truly, God is my salvation,
I trust, I shall not fear.
For the Lord is my strength, my song,
he became my saviour.
With joy you will draw water
from the wells of salvation.
Sing and shout for joy.
for great in your midst is the Holy One of Israel.

(From Isaiah 12)

Gospel: Year A: Matthew 11.2–11; *Year B:* John 1.6–18;
19–28; *Year C:* Luke 3.10–18

A. On the third Sunday in Advent St John the Baptist
remains prominent in the Gospel narrative. In Matthew,
however, the place is no longer on the banks of the
Jordan but the prison in the inaccessible mountainous
region of Perea overlooking the Dead Sea where John is
held captive by Herod Antipas. It would seem that John,
no doubt sensing that his own death was imminent,
looked for confirmation of his earlier declaration at the
very start of Jesus' public ministry, that Jesus was the
Lamb of God who takes away the sin of the world, and so
he sent messengers to Christ to ask for this assurance.
Jesus replied by citing the words of the prophet Isaiah,
who had described the signs by which God would accredit
the true Messiah: 'the eyes of the blind shall be opened,
the ears of the deaf unsealed, the lame shall leap like a
deer and the tongues of the dumb sing for joy' – the very
miracles that Jesus had been performing (Isaiah 35.5).

Jesus then used the occasion to speak of John the
Baptist whom he praised for his ascetic lifestyle, proclaim-
ing him the greatest of all the prophets of Israel, indeed
the greatest man who had ever lived. He affirmed also
that John was the prophet whom the people had been led
to expect as the forerunner of the Messiah, the one of
whom John's father, Zechariah, filled with the Holy
Spirit, had said, 'And you, little child, you shall be called
Prophet of the Most High, for you will go before the Lord
to prepare the way for him' (Luke 1.76). Jesus added that
the least in the kingdom of heaven would be greater than
John the Baptist. This remark is our Lord's confirmation
that the baptism he would give is superior to John's.

B. Today's Gospel reading begins with three verses from
the Prologue to St John's Gospel. These verses affirm that
a man called John had come to be a witness to the light
that was about to break upon the world. The reading then

moves on to the beginning of the Gospel narrative. The
Pharisees had sent messengers to John the Baptist to ask
on what authority he was baptizing. Was he the Messiah?
The questions put by the priests and Levites show that
their concept of the Messiah remained confined within
the concept of the typical Old Testament prophet. The
notion of a radical transfiguration on human nature,
accomplished by the Spirit of God, was beyond them.

John protested strongly that he was not the Messiah
and that he was much inferior to the Messiah, who was
still to come. John said, 'I baptize with water.' He might
have said, 'only with water'; and then in the verses that
follow today's reading he explains that the Messiah's
baptism will be with the Holy Spirit. John knew that the
repentance which his baptism demanded could not burn
out the source of evil in the human heart; salvation could
come to mankind only through the re-creative power of
God himself.

When Jesus said that the least in the kingdom of heaven
would be greater than even John the Baptist, he was
speaking of the incomparable status that his gift of the
Holy Spirit would confer on those incorporated into his
body through baptism. They would become truly his kins-
folk, sharing divine life.

C. John the Baptist's preaching evoked an immediate
response from the crowd which comprised people from
every walk of life – even some Pharisees and Sadducees
had followed John to the banks of the Jordan, as Matthew
tells us. They had taken seriously his announcement of
the imminence of the Day of the Lord and its attendant
retribution and cried out, 'What must we do to be saved?'

Perhaps his answer disappointed them; they may have
expected him to propose some kind of extraordinary acts
of penance; he simply reiterated the ancient prophetic
call to act with love and justice and keep the fundamental
laws of God. Centuries earlier Isaiah had denounced
theatrical self-affliction – hanging the head and lying

down in ashes – as mere counterfeits of real repentance. John proclaimed that genuine repentance is the only preparation for entry into the kingdom of the Messiah he could only call to repentance. The fact that there was a feeling of such high expectancy amongst the people demonstrates that the popular concept of the Messiah, like that of the priests and Levites mentioned in St John's Gospel, did not extend beyond the Old Testament category of the prophet; but John insisted that, like all of the prophets of old, the Messiah, the Son of God, alone could confer the life of the Spirit.

Advent 4

Old Testament thought:
The maiden is with child and will soon give birth to a son
whom she will call Immanuel,
a name which means 'God is with us'.   (Isaiah 7.14)

Vocal prayer:
  I will sing for ever of your love, O Lord;
through all ages my mouth will proclaim your truth.
Of this I am sure, that your love lasts for ever,
that your truth is firmly established as the heavens.
I have made a covenant with my chosen one;
I have sworn to David my servant:
I will establish your dynasty for ever
and set up your throne through all ages.
  I will sing for ever of your love, O Lord.

(From Psalm 89)

Gospel: Year A: Matthew 1.18–25; *Year B:* Luke 1.26–38; *Year C:* Luke 1.39–44

Note. In each liturgical cycle a different Gospel reading is provided for Sunday Advent 4. All tell of the mystery of the incarnation, but each highlights a different aspect of it.

A. In meditating upon this Gospel we approach the mystery of the incarnation from Joseph's point of view. Joseph was a devout and kindly man. When he discovered that Mary, his betrothed, was pregnant he felt obliged, no doubt out of respect for Jewish law, to break off the betrothal contract; but while judging the circumstances according to law, he refrained from becoming censorious and decided to settle the matter privately so that Mary would not suffer ignominy. Like his celebrated namesake in the Old Testament, he then received enlightenment in a dream. The child Mary now carried had been conceived by direct divine intervention. Joseph was therefore to take Mary as his wife and care for her and the child, just as Joseph in Egypt had become the provider for the ancient family of God.

Some theologians argue that the Child could have somehow, by later divine intervention, become the Son of God even if Joseph had been the natural Father. Such speculation directly contradicts the view that the early Church expressed in the creeds by the phrase, 'born of the Virgin Mary' and contradicts also the very plain affirmation of St John, who writes that the Word made flesh was 'born not of human stock or urge of the flesh or will of man but of God himself' (John 1.13).

Later reflection by the Church on the mystery of Mary's motherhood is a working out of the implications of the fact that the flesh assumed by the Word came from his mother, Mary.

B. In this cycle meditation begins with attention to Mary's mind and mood. She too must have been supremely devout; indeed she was the end-product of Jewish piety, and the annunciation scene was a climax in a life of habitual prayer. Like all in the Old Testament who received angelic visitation she trembled when the divine messenger addressed her. She knew that it is a fearful thing to fall into the hands of God, to be called to collaborate in the divine purpose, as the fictional Judith – 'the Jewess' – had learned when called to destroy her people's persecutor. We are struck by Mary's caution: only after she had probed the angel's credentials, learning that the plan he proposed was in line with the way God had operated in the past through women like Sarah and others, did she consent to co-operate. And she did co-operate; of her own free will she undertook to become the mother of the divine Word. The acclaim addressed to the heroine Judith is more appropriately addressed to Mary: 'By doing this with your own hand you have deserved well of Israel' (Judith 15.10).

Giving an explanation of the divine plan, the angel recalled also the Messianic promises to King David. Mary's child would sit on David's throne, but his kingdom would extend beyond earth's boundaries; it would be an everlasting kingdom.

C. In cycle A the Gospel emphasized the mystery of the Word's taking flesh from the Virgin Mary; in cycle B the Gospel introduced the theme of Mary's active part in the plan of salvation, and spoke also of the fulfilment of the Messianic promises; in cycle C the mood is that of pure adoration. The child in Mary's womb is hailed as Lord by the child in Elizabeth's womb and by Elizabeth. Centuries earlier the ark of the covenant, the precious box carrying the Ten Words, had been housed for three months in the hill country of Judea where Elizabeth and Zachariah now lived, and on taking this ark back to Jerusalem King David had danced with joy before this symbol of God's presence; now John the Baptist, last of the Old Testament prophets, leapt with joy in his mother's womb, aware that he was in the presence of the Ark of the New Covenant, Mary, bearing within her womb not the Ten Words of God but the Word himself.

Christmas Day

Old Testament thought:
The people that walked in darkness has seen a great light.
(Isaiah 9.1)

Vocal prayer:
O sing a new song to the Lord,
sing to the Lord all the earth.

    Today a saviour has been born to us.
Let the heavens rejoice and earth be glad,
let the sea and all within it thunder praise,
let the land and all it bears rejoice.

    Today a saviour has been born to us.
All the trees of the wood, shout for joy
at the presence of the Lord for he comes,
he comes to rule the earth.

    Today a saviour has been born to us;
he is Christ the Lord.
(From Psalm 96)

Gospel: Year A: Matthew 1.18–25; *Year B:* Luke 2.1–20;
Year C: John 1.1–18

ABC. Matthew and Luke tell of our Lord's birth in a way
which provides a pictorial focus for meditation, and most
Christians are so familiar with the story that they are able
to summon up images of the Nativity without even
renewed reading of the biblical text. For meditation on
the mystery of the Nativity we could select almost any
excerpt from the Gospel narratives. St John, however,
whose account is not a historical record of what happened
at Bethlehem and contains no imagery relating to that
event, alerts us to what is essential in the Christmas
mystery. In clear and unambiguous language he tells us
who the Child is, who is now lying in that manger.

> The Word was made flesh,
> he lived among us,
> and we saw his glory,
> the glory that is his as the only Son of the Father,
> full of grace and truth (John 1.14).

The infant in the crib is the second Person of the Blessed
Trinity – the Son, the Wisdom, or the Word, of God. As
the Nicene Creed proclaims: he is 'the only Son of God,
eternally begotten of the Father, God from God, Light
from Light, begotten, not made, of one being with the
Father. Through him all things were made.'

Whichever part of the Christmas story we choose as
stimulus to meditation, our prayer ought to be controlled
by St John's affirmation. Bowing before the Infant in the
crib we are not simply rejoicing at the sight of a new
human life, but are adoring God. As St John reminds us
also, no one has ever seen God, and yet in this child he
has assumed our flesh so that we now have a means of
communication with him. In Christ's words we will hear
the words of God the Father: in his actions we will see the
perfect expression of the heart of God the Father.

The Holy Family

Old Testament thought:
Whoever respects his father is atoning for his sins,
he who honours his mother is like someone amassing a
    fortune.   (Ecclesiasticus 3.4–5)

Vocal prayer:
Now, Master, you can let your servant go in peace,
just as you promised;
because my eyes have seen the salvation
which you have prepared for all the nations to see,
a light to enlighten the pagans
and the glory of your people Israel.

(Luke 2.29–32)

Gospel: Year A: Matthew 2.13–15; *Year B:* Luke 2.22–40; *Year C:* Luke 2.41–52

ABC. Most races have revered the family, seeing it as the basic cell of society. The people of Israel possessed this reverence in a high degree. One of the ten absolute laws revealed through Moses was: 'Honour your father and your mother'. This law was not designed to encourage the subjugation of children, but contained the notion that the child's reverence for its parents reflected the reverence all mankind owe to God the Creator; and for their part the parents' love for their children was to be a sign of God's love for us all.

On Christmas Day our meditation centred on the mystery of God's becoming man; on the feast of the Holy Family it is made clear that this mystery was contrived not simply for our admiration but for our benefit. 'For us men and for our salvation he came down from heaven and was made man.' God's presence in a human body was not, so to speak, a self-contained mystery but a source of power from which redemption flowed out into the human race. The divine child had become a real member of a real human family.

Redemption had begun in the creation of a family, and that family was holy because at its heart lived the Son of God. All of our families can become holy to the extent that Christ lives in them; and he comes to live there in response to our prayer and our use of the sacraments he has given us. Because the family is the fundamental human society, the primary means by which the redemption of the world is accomplished is the prayer through which we sanctify our families, prayer which includes family prayer and individual private prayer.

The ultimate purpose of the Incarnation is to form the human race into one great family, God's family, by uniting all human flesh with the Body of Christ through the power of the Holy Spirit, thus drawing all mankind into the life of the Blessed Trinity.

Additional considerations for Years A, B, and C, separately

A. The flight from Bethlehem into Egypt, the sojourn in a foreign land, and the return home to Nazareth when the child's life was no longer threatened, present our imagination with a picture we can well understand. In these events we see the Holy Family enduring the discomforts and dangers that many families experience. The Holy Family was a real family. The evangelist's primary purpose was not, however, to give a naturalistic account of a family's experiences but to show how God's salvific plan was being completed. The Holy Family were recapitulating the plan of salvation: Israel of old had escaped from famine in Canaan and found shelter in Egypt, returning home later to take up permanent residence in the Promised Land; now the Holy Family, nucleus of the new Israel, was re-living the experience of the old Israel, and the salvation of all mankind was about to be accomplished.

B. After the people of Israel had settled in the Promised Land their life centred in the worship of God in the temple. Jesus, carried by Mary and Joseph, entered his temple, for he was Lord of the temple, to be greeted by the devout who awaited his coming, represented by Simeon and Hannah. In spite of his Lordship over the temple Jesus submitted to the law's demands. The parents offered the thanksgiving sacrifice – two young pigeons – paying also the redemption price with which the first-born was bought back from God.

But there is irony here. As Simeon's prophecy revealed, this child was destined to suffer, as was his mother. The payment of the redemption price did not really buy him back – as Isaac was reprieved when a lamb was found caught in a thicket – for this child, some years later, was to be the lamb that was sacrificed.

C. The presentation of the child in the temple foreshadowed his death on the cross; the finding of the twelve-year-old boy in the temple was a veiled allusion to his rising from the dead to enter into the presence of his Father in heaven. Mary and Joseph searched for him 'among their relations and acquaintances', and were perplexed and a little aggrieved when, on discovering him in the temple, he said, 'I must be busy with my Father's affairs'. He was moving out now into a greater family than the folk at Nazareth.

The picture of Jesus asking and answering questions amongst the learned is significant. By this scene we are taught that Jesus was able to answer serious questions with authority, for he was of one substance with God the Father, the source of all truth, but at the same time we are being shown how, as man, he was willing to learn. Although he was true God he did not allow divine status to over-rule human finitude for he had 'emptied himself ... and became as men are' (Philippians 2.7). One way in which he demonstrated this self-emptying was by his readiness to ask questions. Although he would never fall into error, he had to learn by the methods that men and women employ; and as man he learned perfectly.

Returning with Mary and Joseph to Nazareth after being found in the temple he continued to realize his self-emptying by the humility with which he subjected himself to family discipline exercised by Mary and Joseph.

Mary Mother of God

Old Testament thought:
You are the glory of Jerusalem!
You are the great pride of Israel!
You are the highest glory of our race!   (Judith 14.9)

Vocal prayer:
May you be blessed, my daughter, by God most high,
beyond all women on earth;
and may the Lord be blessed,
the Creator of heaven and earth,
by whose guidance you cut off the head
of the leader of our enemies.
The trust you have shown
shall not pass from the memories of men,
but shall ever remind them
of the power of God.   (Judith 13.18–19)

Gospel: Luke 2.16–21

ABC. On Christmas Day our interest was directed to our Lord's divinity. The infant in the crib was no less than the second Person of the Blessed Trinity. On the octave of Christmas our interest is directed to his humanity. Although God, he is also true man. We impress this fact upon our minds by dwelling on the thought that Mary was his real mother. To call Mary the Mother of God is another way of professing our belief in the incarnation of the Word. All of the doctrines that have been proclaimed about Mary are commentaries on the mystery of the Incarnation.

The fact that Mary was truly the mother of the Word is virtually denied by some kinds of popular devotion. The hymn, for example, that speaks of 'the one spotless womb wherein Jesus was laid' is misleading, for Jesus was not laid in Mary's womb, but made from it. She was no surrogate mother into whom a divine infant had been implanted, but his natural mother. In the fourth century this false notion was repudiated by Athanasius who wrote: 'Gabriel did not say, "what is born in you", in case it might be thought that the body had been introduced into her from outside; he said, "what is born of you", so that it would be accepted that what she gave birth to, came from her in the natural way'. The flesh of our Lord Jesus was Mary's flesh, and because in this way he had taken human flesh upon himself, all that he did thereafter was done in our behalf. It was 'for us men and for our salvation' that he had come down from heaven and become man.

There is another thought, however, that is bound to enter our minds when we meditate upon the reality of Mary's divine motherhood. The first object of which every baby becomes aware is its mother's face. So it was with the Son of God. He looked upon Mary's face as every child looks upon its mother's face, and he reacted to her as every child reacts to its mother. He called out to her to satisfy his infant needs, and he relied upon her as a child and as a youth for his initial religious and moral training. Because he is flesh of our flesh and bone of our bone, the relationship he had with his mother, he has bequeathed to us. As he turned to her in his infant need, so we may and should turn to her with the childlike spirit that Jesus exhorted us to acquire. If we seek Mary's intercession she will lead us to him.

The Epiphany

Old Testament thought:
Thus says the Lord
to him whose life is despised:
kings will stand up when they see you,
and princes will bow.   (Isaiah 49.7)

Vocal prayer:
    O Lord, hear my prayer,
    let my cry for help reach you;
do not hide your face from me
when I am in trouble;
bend down to listen to me,
when I call, be quick to answer me!
    O Lord, hear my prayer,
    let my cry for help reach you.   (Psalm 102.1–2)

Gospel: Matthew 2.1–12

The feast of the Epiphany links the mystery of our Lord's divinity with the mystery of his humanity, teaching us to adore the royalty of divine majesty by bowing down before the helplessness of an infant. The three kings, the magi, represent the power, the wealth, and the wisdom of this world, when it has cast off all trace of arrogance and self-seeking. The adoration of the magi speaks of power gained by perceiving the might hidden in the weakness of this child, of wealth that accrues from compassion, and of wisdom that blossoms by submission to the teaching of Christ.

The adoration of the magi is a dramatized commentary on St Paul's words: 'His state was divine, yet he did not cling to his equality with God but emptied himself ... even to accepting death, death on a cross. But God raised him high so that all beings ... should bend the knee at the name of Jesus ...' (Philippians 2.6–10). Our faith and worship become genuine only when we recognize the glory of the Son of God in the meekness of the child in the manger and in the desolation of the Man of Sorrows on the cross. The shadow of the cross falls even upon the manger of Bethlehem, and behind the picture of the three kings kneeling devoutly before the child lurks the spectre of a fourth king – Herod.

Our Lord's self-emptying, to become the Suffering Servant of the Lord, is the model for the disciple. The passage quoted above from St Paul begins with the sentence: 'In your minds you must be the same as Christ Jesus ...' (Philippians 2.5). It is not enough to recognize the glory of God in the meekness and sufferings of Christ. We must imitate his gentleness and meekness if we wish to become bearers of his glory, and extend his kingdom in the world. The vocation of disciple is hard but St Peter tells us that we will be given strength to carry it out: 'By his divine power he has given us all the things we need for life and for true devotion ... you will be able to share the divine nature ...' (2 Peter 1.3–4).

The Baptism of our Lord

Old Testament thought:
On him the spirit of the Lord rests,
a spirit of wisdom and insight,
a spirit of counsel and power,
a spirit of knowledge and of the fear of the Lord.

(Isaiah 11.2)

Vocal prayer:
O give the Lord you sons of God,
give the Lord glory and power,
give the Lord the glory of his name.
Adore the Lord in his holy court.
The Lord's voice resounding on the waters,
the Lord on the immensity of waters;
the voice of the Lord, full of power,
the voice of the Lord, full of splendour.
The God of glory thunders.
In his temple they all cry: 'Glory!'
The Lord sat enthroned over the flood;
the Lord sits as king for ever.   (Psalm 29)

Gospel: Year A: Matthew 3.13–17; *Year B:* Mark 1.7–11;
Year C: Luke 3.15–16, 21–2

ABC. Bringing the Christmas season to a close, in each cycle the Liturgy of the Word presents us with a Gospel figuring John the Baptist who is about to retire before the rising of the true light, whose baptism will supersede John's baptism. Like the Easter season, which is followed immediately by the feast of the Blessed Trinity, so Christmas is rounded off by the celebration of a feast which is indeed a feast of the Trinity, for in the feast of the Baptism of our Lord not only do we see the Son, the Word made flesh, in centre stage, but see also a symbol of the Holy Spirit descending upon him, and then hear the voice of the Father acknowledging the Son.

John tried to dissuade Jesus from submitting to his baptism, but Jesus insisted, for he wanted to demonstrate his solidarity with the human race for whose sake he had been – in St Paul's words – 'made sin'. He had not been made to sin, but to take upon himself all of the consequences of mankind's sin, and because the wages of sin are death, so by descending into the Jordan river he signified his going down into death.

The baptism of Jesus was first of all an action-prophecy of his death; next by his rising out of the water it foretold his rising from the dead; and finally the descent of the Holy Spirit spoke of the breathing of the Spirit upon the Twelve and his manifestation in power on the day of Pentecost. The baptism scene can therefore be regarded as a prologue to the Gospel story. In it Jesus set out the overall plan of his mission.

The fact that the Holy Spirit was seen descending in *bodily form* is significant. As the eternal Son of God our Lord never ceased to be in union with the Father through the Spirit, but having genuinely assumed a human nature he had to experience the indwelling of the Spirit in the same mode as men and women experience him, so that after his dying and rising he could hand on the Spirit in the same mode to mankind. At his baptism in the Jordan river the Holy Spirit was seen therefore descending upon him in *bodily form.*

Just as our Lord's baptism in Jordan foreshadowed the entire paschal mystery, so Christian baptism, by which the gift of the Spirit is first given to men and women, points back to that same paschal mystery and makes it effectively present.

Lent 1

Old Testament thought:
Seek the Lord while he is still to be found,
call to him while he is still near.
Let the wicked man abandon his way,
the evil man his thoughts.
Let him turn back to the Lord who will take pity on him,
to our God who is rich in forgiving.   (Isaiah 55.6–7)

Vocal prayer:
Have mercy on me, O God, in your goodness,
in your great tenderness wipe away my faults;
wash me clean of my guilt,
purify me from my sin.
For I am well aware of my faults,
I have my sin always in mind,
having sinned against none other than you.
God, create a clean heart in me,
put into me a new and constant spirit,
do not banish me from your presence,
do not deprive me of your holy spirit.
Have mercy on us, Lord, for we have sinned.

(From Psalm 51)

Gospel: Year A: Matthew 4.1–11; *Year B:* Mark 1.12–15; *Year C:* Luke 4.1–13

ABC. The Spirit descended upon Jesus at his baptism in the Jordan *in bodily form*, in the way, that is, in which the Spirit was to be given to men and women when Jesus had finished the work he was sent to do; and it was now in his human nature that Jesus required the help of the Holy Spirit, in order to persevere in and complete his mission. Immediately following his baptism Jesus was urged by the Spirit to go into the wilderness of Judea where, in suffering temptation by the Devil, he proved that his human nature was real and no myth; it made him vulnerable to all the temptations that assail men and women. But he differs from all of us in that he never yielded to temptation; thus he is the perfect model for our imitation.

But he is more than our model; he is also the means that enables us to succeed in our attempt at imitating him. His human nature was joined with his divinity, so that rising from the dead, having conquered the power of the Tempter by his sacrifice on the cross, he was able to hand on to us a share in the divine life which had sustained his humanity in his battle with the Devil.

In establishing his kingdom, that is, the rule of God in the hearts and minds of men and women, Jesus set about the task in a way that did not diminish the handicap that his human nature brought with it. The three temptations described by the evangelists can be taken as representative of three different kinds of temptation, but more significant is what they have in common. Each one in its own context shows Jesus being tempted to overrule his humanity. The Devil suggests that he could win the allegiance of mankind by miraculously satisfying all their earthly needs and desires; or by compromising with evil – worshipping him; or by performing some outstanding miracle – jumping down from the pinnacle of the temple.

By adopting any such method of winning the obedience of men and women Jesus would have been using a false

means to gain his end. He had been given a human
nature so that through the sacrifice of a sinless one he
could offer to the Father the obedience that mankind had
refused. The Devil's three temptations in the wilderness
were a preview of his final temptation on the cross, when
the Devil's taunt was uttered again: 'If you are the Son of
God, save yourself and us'. To be true to his mission he
dared not invoke his divinity to get him off the hook: he
had to remain true man to the bitter end. The Father
rewarded this faith, and we are the beneficiaries, for
through his privation we have been given a share in the
life of the Blessed Trinity.

Lent 2

Old Testament thought:
When Moses came down from the mountain of Sinai
he did not know that the skin on his face was radiant
after speaking with the Lord.   (Exodus 34.29)

Vocal prayer:
The Lord is my light and my help,
whom shall I fear?
The Lord is the stronghold of my life
before whom shall I shrink?
It is your face, O Lord, that I seek;
hide not your face.
Dismiss not your servant in anger;
you have been my help.
I am sure I shall see the Lord's goodness
in the land of the living.
Hope in him, hold firm and take heart.
Hope in the Lord!   (From Psalm 27)

Gospel: Year A: Matthew 17.1–9; *Year B:* Mark 9.2–10;
Year C: Luke 9.28–36

ABC. The ascent of Jesus with the Twelve of a mountain
in Galilee – possibly Tabor – marks a decisive turning
point in their itinerary. Having proclaimed the gospel
mainly in his native province of Galilee, Jesus now turned
his face resolutely towards Jerusalem where he would
crown his proclamation with the offering up of his life. On
the summit of this mountain Jesus granted the inner
circle of disciples – Peter, James and John – a vision,
designed to prepare them for the events that lay ahead,
and in a measure to interpret these events.

The three disciples saw Jesus' face shining like the sun,
as Moses' face had shone after he spoke with the Lord;
but on the mountain Jesus was revealed to them as
greater than Moses: not only his face but his clothing, his
whole person, was irradiated with heavenly brightness.
Seeing this sign of their Master's exaltation above Moses,
the apostles were being led to understand better the
meaning of his sonship with the Father. The heavenly
brightness of the vision was also a preview of the resurrection glory into which Jesus would enter after his
passion and death.

The vision then moved into another phase. Jesus was
seen talking with Moses and Elijah. This scene impressed
upon the apostles the validity of the Old Testament
witness to Jesus as the Messiah; it also pointed to a similarity between Jesus and these two great prophets. Both
had suffered much: Moses from the burden of delivering
the people from Egypt and sharing in the trials in the
wilderness, and from the people's rebelliousness; Elijah
from persecution by an apostate king. The link with the
prophets hinted therefore at our Lord's passion and
death. But Moses and Elijah had departed this life in
mystery: Moses, as his strength failed, climbed up Mount
Nebo, never to return, and no one ever found his grave;
Elijah was seen to vanish into the heavens on a chariot.

This was a further adumbration of our Lord's resurrection.

Following this revelation of the inseparable link between suffering and glory, which characterizes the paschal mystery, Peter and James and John were filled with fear, but the Father's voice sounded from a cloud that concealed his glory and yet radiated brightness. The Father confirmed the profession that Peter had made so recently: Jesus was indeed the Son of the most high God and if they only listened to him, that is, believed in him, trusted his promises, and obeyed his commands, they could face the future without fear.

Lent 3

Old Testament thought:
The Lord said to Moses: 'You must strike the rock, and water will flow from it for the people to drink.'
(Exodus 17.6)

Vocal prayer:
O God, my God, for you I long
for you my soul is thirsting.
My body pines for you
like a dry, weary land without water.
So I gaze on you in the sanctuary
to see your strength and your glory.
For your love is better than life,
my lips will speak your praise.
So I will bless you all my life,
in your name I will lift up my hands.
My soul shall be filled as with a banquet,
my mouth shall praise you with joy.   (Psalm 63)

Gospel: John 4.5–42

ABC. His encounter with a Samaritan woman gave Jesus a perfect opportunity to teach about mankind's longing for Truth and eternal life.

Water is a symbol of life, and the thirst for water a powerful symbol for mankind's thirst for Truth and for eternal life. Jesus saw the woman as a personification first of her nation, and second of the whole of humanity. At first the woman took his words literally, thinking he was going to provide her with an easy method of getting her daily supply of water, but Jesus led her to understand that he was speaking metaphorically about eternal life; the woman responded, expressing a desire to have this water.

When she asked him how to obtain this water of life Jesus appeared to change the subject, but he did not, for he began to speak about worship, which is a direct manifestation of the reception of the Holy Spirit. The woman's next response confirms this because as soon as Jesus asked about her husbands, she told him that her people worshipped on Mount Gerizim. What had her husbands to do with worship?

In 2 Kings 17.24–34 we learn how Samaria was resettled with Babylonians after the overthrow of the kingdom of Israel. The incomers, we are told, brought with them five gods from five cities. These *baalim*, were the people's 'lords' or 'husbands'. The settlers tried to marry the worship of their own 'husbands' with Israel's worship of the true 'Lord'; they even celebrated a modified form of the Passover. These were the five former husbands and the one present non-husband to which Jesus referred; and that is why the woman answered Jesus' enquiry about her husbands by saying: 'Our fathers worshipped on this mountain, while you say that Jerusalem is the place one ought to worship'. Jesus told her that both her nation's form of worship and that of his own people would be superseded by worship in spirit and truth. In response, the woman showed a genuine longing for the

~ coming of the Messiah, and Jesus declared that he was that Messiah.

The incident ends therefore on a note of hope. The woman, seen now not just as a Samaritan but as a personification of all mankind, becomes a sign of the potential in every man and woman for thirst after the water of eternal life. The disciples returned and were astonished to find Jesus in conversation with a Samaritan. From this they were to learn that the field of their future labours was the whole world, in which they would have to spread the Good News and mediate the life of the Spirit to all mankind.

Lent 4

Old Testament thought:
A flood was rising from the earth
and watering all the surface of the soil.
God fashioned man of dust from the soil.
Then he breathed into his nostrils a breath of life.
(Genesis 2.6–7)

Vocal prayer:
My soul is thirsting for God,
the God of my life;
when can I enter and see
the face of God?
Send out your light and your truth,
let these be my guide,
to lead me to your holy mountain
and to the place where you live.
Then I shall go to the altar of God,
to the God of my joy,
I shall rejoice, I shall praise you on the harp,
O Lord, my God.
(From Psalms 42, 43)

Gospel: John 9.1–41

ABC. The cure of the man born blind is the sixth of the seven signs recorded in St John's Gospel. These signs were genuine physical miracles, but all pointed beyond what was seen to a spiritual reality. On one occasion (John 6.26) Jesus upbraided the disciples because while rejoicing in the physical benefit of his miraculous provision of bread they had remained blind to the sign this miracle gave them.

When he cured the man born blind Jesus contradicted the popular Jewish notion that illness was the result of some actual sin. The reason for this man's blindness was so that God might be glorified. The cure of the man would indeed give glory to God alone, for congenital blindness was considered curable only through divine intervention. By curing this man Jesus was revealing himself as one with God the Father; and the gestures he used in the process were designed to make clear this oneness with God the Father, for they recall the account in Genesis chapter 2, where mankind is seen being formed out of moist earth and the infusion of breath from the mouth of God. Jesus was being glorified as the Word through whom all things were made, and who, now incarnate in the man Jesus, was alone capable of remaking mankind, now spiritually congenitally blind as a result of the Fall.

Reading this account today we are meant to understand the man's congenital blindness as a symbol for original sin. Our Lord's next action confirms this view, for he sent the man to wash in the pool of Siloam, an action that would complete his cure. This part of the incident is an allusion to the sacrament of baptism which removes the guilt of original sin.

In the conclusion of the incident we see the man being confirmed in his faith. Having had his sight restored – as the Christian is enlightened in baptism – he acknowledged Jesus as the 'Son of Man' that is the Messiah, the anointed one of God who was to come to redeem the world. Finally Jesus condemned some of the Pharisees for their arrogant self-assurance. They stubbornly hung on to their interpretation of details of the Law – in this case the Sabbath law – in face of clear evidence given by the deeds of Jesus. This was culpable blindness.

Lent 5

Old Testament thought:
I mean to raise you from your graves,
and I shall put my spirit in you, and you will live,
and I shall resettle you on your own soil.

(Ezekiel 37.12–14)

Vocal prayer:
Out of the depths I cry to you, O Lord,
Lord, hear my voice!
O let your ears be attentive
to the voice of my pleading.
My soul is waiting for the Lord,
I count on his word.
My soul is longing for the Lord
more than watchman for daybreak.
Because with the Lord there is mercy
and fullness of redemption,
Israel indeed he will redeem
from all its iniquities.

(From Psalm 130)

Gospel: John 11.1–45

ABC. The raising of Lazarus, the last sign recorded in St John's Gospel, foreshadows our Lord's death and resurrection. It is a sign also that men and women who believe will be given a share in his resurrection-life. It teaches that resurrection-life is more than resuscitation. Lazarus was resuscitated but in the end he died as all people do. If to be 'raised up' – a phrase used in the liturgy of the Anointing of the Sick – is no more than to be resuscitated, that is no genuine Good News. The miracle of the raising of Lazarus and the dialogue contained in the narrative reveal the meaning of resurrection.

The Old Testament provides a clue. Ezekiel saw a heap of bones being reassembled and infused with life. The vision announces that the people were about to be enlivened by his Spirit and led back into their homeland where, in a spirit of repentance for the nation's past sins, they would resume worship in the temple, while leading lives according to the Lord's commandments. Resurrection, symbolized by the reassembling of the bones, was essentially the inauguration of a new penitent but joyful life in the power of God's Spirit. The raising of Lazarus was a genuine physical miracle, but it was also a vision, comparable with that of Ezekiel, of the essence of resurrection. Resurrection life is redeemed life, a life free from sin. Our Lord's last words in this episode confirm this: 'Unbind him, let him go free [from sin]'.

The resurrection-life begins now. Our Lord hinted strongly at the here-and-now quality of the resurrection when he said to Martha, who thought only of the resurrection at the end of time, 'I am the resurrection'. St Paul stresses this aspect of resurrection in Romans from which the second reading of this Sunday is taken. 'You are interested', he writes, 'in the spiritual, since the Spirit of God has made his home in you.' He continues to explain that the mortal body, though dead, if progressively sanctified during this life will eventually enjoy everlasting life.

'Though your body may be dead it is because of sin, but if Christ is in you then your spirit is life itself because you have been justified; and if the Spirit of him who raised Jesus from the dead is living in you, then he who raised Jesus from the dead will give life to your own mortal bodies through his Spirit living in you' (Romans 8.9–11).

Lent 6 (Passion Sunday/Palm Sunday)

Old Testament thought:
Rejoice heart and soul, daughter of Zion!
Shout with gladness, daughter of Jerusalem!
See now, your king comes to you;
he is victorious, he is triumphant,
humble and riding on a donkey.   (Zechariah 9.9)

Vocal prayer:
Lord, make your ways known to me,
teach me your paths.
Set me in the way of your truth, and teach me,
for you are the God who saves me.
All day long I hope in you
because of your goodness, Lord.
Remember your kindness, Lord,
your love that you showed long ago.
Do not remember the sins of my youth;
but rather, with your love remember me.
All the Lord's paths are love and truth
for those who keep his covenant and decrees.
For the sake of your name, Lord,
forgive my guilt, for it is great.

(From Psalm 25)

Gospel: Year A: Matthew 21.1–11; *Year B:* Mark 11.1–10; *Year C:* Luke 19.28–40.

ABC. On Passion Sunday, or Palm Sunday as it is usually called, the Mass is introduced by the account of our Lord's entry into Jerusalem. The manner of his entry matched perfectly the prophecy of Zechariah who had foretold that the Messiah would enter his royal city seated upon the 'foal of a donkey'. And so when Jesus began his approach to Jerusalem from the Mount of Olives, mounted upon a donkey, the word spread like wildfire throughout the city and surrounding countryside that the Messiah was at last coming to them. Fired with patriotic zeal the populace rushed out to welcome him with shouts of 'Hosannah to the son of David'. They had recognized the signal that he was the Messiah but failed to understand the significance of his being seated upon a beast of burden and not upon a war-horse. At the end of the week this same crowd, disillusioned because of his failure to satisfy their worldly expectations, were shouting: 'Crucify him'.

In preparation for our meditation on the great events of Holy Week we ought to ask ourselves if we are not tainted with the fickleness of that Palm Sunday crowd, our love for our Lord being in some measure cupboard-love, and our practice of our faith aimed at gaining assurance of material comfort.

Having made this preparation we can then devote all our effort – beginning as early as possible in Holy Week – to deeper penetration of the paschal mysteries, to *The Hour of Jesus*. That *Hour* had three moments: the Last Supper, the Passion, the Resurrection. While attending to each moment separately we must not however lose sight of the fact that the accomplishment of our Lord's task – the redemption of mankind – required that all three moments formed a single Hour, the one paschal mystery.

The Hour of Jesus

1. Holy Thursday

Old Testament thought:
This day is to be a day of remembrance for you,
and you must celebrate it as a feast in the Lord's honour.
For all generations you are to declare it a day of festival,
    for ever. (Exodus 12.14)

Vocal prayer:
How can I repay the Lord
for his goodness to me?
The cup of salvation I will raise;
    I will call on the Lord's name.
O precious in the eyes of the Lord
is the death of his faithful.
Your servant, Lord, your servant am I;
you have loosened my bonds.
A thanksgiving sacrifice I make:
    I will call on the Lord's name.
My vows to the Lord I will fulfil
before all his people. (From Psalm 116)

Gospel: John 13.1–15

ABC. The celebration of the whole paschal mystery, which was the consummation of God the Father's scheme of redemption, begins with the celebration of our Lord's institution, at his Last Passover Supper, of the holy eucharist. This is most appropriate, for at the Last Supper, in the long discourse that we can read in John's Gospel chapters 13 to 18, Jesus interpreted God's redemptive plan, which ended with his own sacrifice on the cross and subsequent rising from the tomb.

At the Last Supper Jesus not only provided for all time a commentary on his historical passion, death, and resurrection, but by instituting the eucharist as a perpetual celebration of these events – just as Moses had instituted the Passover as a 'day of festival for ever' – provided also a means that ensured the perpetual efficacy of that paschal mystery. The eucharist was a memorial of his once and for all dying and glorification and at the same time a making present his once and for ever sacrifice.

The letter to Hebrews (in chapter 9) speaks of this eternal dimension of our Lord's sacrifice when it tells us that our Lord has passed through 'the greater, the more perfect tent', and in the heavenly sanctuary of the Father's presence has 'offered himself as the perfect sacrifice to God through the eternal Spirit'. This sacrifice through the eternal Spirit is identical with the historical sacrifice on Calvary.

When week by week or day by day we celebrate the holy eucharist we become mystically present therefore both at Calvary and in the heavenly sanctuary, for Christ brings his people with him into the Father's presence. The eucharist is indeed a gate into heaven.

This heavenly ambience is created at the celebration of the eucharist by our Lord's presence – his real presence, for the Lord who is present in the bread and wine of the eucharist is the risen and glorified Lord. In physically consuming the eucharistic body and blood of our Lord, that which is eternal in us – the resurrection body that is to be – is nourished by the heavenly substance of the risen Christ.

---

2. Good Friday

Old Testament thought:
If the virtuous man is God's own Son, God will take his
    part
and rescue him from the clutches of his enemies.
Let us test him with cruelty and with torture,
and thus explore this gentleness of his.

(Wisdom 2.18–19)

Vocal prayer:
My God, my God, why have you deserted me?
How far from saving me, the words I groan!
I call all day, my God, but you never answer,
all night long I call and cannot rest.
Yet, Holy One, you
who make your home in the praises of Israel,
in you our fathers put their trust,
they trusted and you rescued them;
they called to you for help and they were saved,
they never trusted you in vain.   (From Psalm 22)

Gospel: John 18.1–19, 42

ABC. The Atonement, the complete reconciliation of the human race with God the Father, was brought about by the mutual glorifying of God the Son and God the Father through the Son's act of perfect obedience in love – his sacrifice on the cross. Our Lord's entire life was an act of loving obedience, but that total oblation to his Father's will was decisively manifested within the three days from Thursday evening until Sunday evening at the end of Holy Week. That was his hour – the Hour of Jesus.

Before enduring agony and death on the cross Jesus suffered by anticipation in the garden of Gethsemane where he went immediately after leaving the Upper Room. His agony there was no less than his agony on the cross. Not only, with divine prescience, was he able to imagine vividly, and to sense fully what was about to befall him, but he also grasped in horror the significance of his suffering. He was being treated as a sinner, the symbol of which was his crucifixion between two terrorists. As St Paul wrote, he was 'made sin for us'. The indignity of being rubbed in all the filth of sin was his agony. In the garden he experienced in full measure all the misery and desolation that can afflict sinful humanity. In addition he experienced the pain of temptation, for he could quite easily have escaped into the hill country of Judea, but he made no attempt to do so.

In the agony in the garden Jesus overcame the instinctive impulse towards self-preservation, and showed the interior submission to the Father's will which had characterized his whole life; and it is this eternal interior sacrifice, manifested exteriorly at a precise moment in time in his death on the cross, that is present every time bread is broken and wine poured out in the celebration of the eucharist.

This act of the sinless Son of God was the converse of the act of disobedience by which the human race had at the beginning defied God its creator, and by it the tables were turned on the powers of evil. The purpose of the Son's action was not that he might gain something, but solely that mankind might be welcomed back into the friendship of God. It could be asked: Why did God the Father not simply forgive mankind? Was it necessary that Jesus should suffer as he did before forgiveness became effective? A complete answer to that question is beyond human comprehension. The Atonement remains a deep mystery; but it is a mystery that makes sense.

Total reconciliation of mankind with God required that mankind's dignity be maintained. It was human nature that had sinned, therefore in justice it was human nature that would have to make satisfaction; but because the offence had been against the divine majesty it was beyond the power of any human being to make adequate satisfaction. Only God can satisfy God. In the eleventh century St Anselm of Canterbury expressed the problem very neatly. He wrote: 'If only God can and man ought to make this satisfaction, then necessarily One must make it who is both God and man.'

When we venerate the cross on Good Friday and meditate upon the mystery of the Atonement we discover that we have returned to the mystery that underlies all of the mysteries of our Faith: the Incarnation. In order to re-make fallen human nature, the Son of God put on the working clothes of human nature and set about a task that required infinite effort. How that repair job on human nature was contrived is a question beyond the capacity of our minds to answer, but it was accomplished at the cost of indescribable pain, the pain of Christ's dying on the cross.

At the beginning of this comment it was said that our Lord's being raised upon the cross was an act wherein he glorified the Father and the Father glorified him. It was an act which expressed the mutual love between the Son and the Father. We may find it hard to grasp how the Father could endure to see the sufferings of his Son on the cross. The explanation is that both Son and Father love mankind; the Father and the Son are one, as Jesus told us. The agony of the Son and the Father's having to behold it are both signs of the infinite love that God has for us men and women.

It was 'for us men and for our salvation' that the Crucifixion took place; and in beholding that event, God the Father saw not only the humanity assumed by his Son but also the humanity of all who, as members of Christ's Body on earth, are moving towards sanctification, and who, through suffering and in the power of the Holy Spirit, become co-workers with Christ in his work of redemption.

> Father, the hour has come:
> glorify your Son
> so that your Son may glorify you;
> and through the power over all mankind that you
>   have given him,
> let him give eternal life to all those you have entrusted
>   to him (John 17.1–2).

3. Easter Sunday

Old Testament thought:
I was thrust down and falling
but the Lord was my helper.   (From Psalm 118)

Vocal prayer:
Truly, God is my salvation,
I trust, I shall not fear.
For the Lord is my strength, my song,
he is my saviour.
With joy you will draw water
from the wells of salvation.
Sing a psalm to the Lord
for he has done glorious deeds,
make them known to all the earth!
People of Zion, sing and shout for joy
for great in your midst
is the Holy One of Israel.   (Isaiah 12.2–6)

Gospel: Matthew 28.1–10; Mark 16.1–7; Luke 24.1–12; John 20.1–9

ABC. Our meditations during Holy Week impressed upon us the fact that only through suffering was our Lord able to enter into his glory; now on Easter Day we take note of the equally important fact that the necessary consummation of the paschal event was his resurrection from the dead. The proclamation of this fact became the foundation and core of the preaching of the early Church, as it must be of the Church today. St Paul affirmed this clearly when he wrote to the Corinthians: 'If Christ has not been raised then our preaching is useless and your believing it is useless; indeed, we are shown up as witnesses who have committed perjury before God, because we swore in evidence before God that he had raised Christ to life' (1 Corinthians 15.14–16). Although the Catholic Faith has given birth to a whole splendid philosophy of life the foundation of that Faith is not a philosophical theory but the fact of the resurrection of Christ, and we believe in that fact on the evidence of witnesses, as St Paul implies. The evidence is contained in the four Gospel passages noted above. While the report of an empty tomb and the vision of angels is common to all Gospels, details vary. These are precisely the kind of variations one would expect to find in the recollection of events by different individuals and groups after the passage of many years. In respect of these variations the Jerusalem Bible comments: 'All this gives the impression that different groups, which cannot now be easily identified, have given rise to different strands of tradition. But these very divergences of tradition are far better witnesses than any artificial or contrived uniformity, to the antiquity of the evidence and the historical quality of these manifestations of the risen Christ.'

Our task this week is to focus our minds upon, and seek to become present at, the greatest event of all time: the resurrection of Christ. We can choose any of the Gospels and meditate on the happening as a whole or upon any detail in the story that specially appeals to us. We should constantly remind ourselves that when we join in the celebration of the eucharist we are in the presence of the risen Christ.

Easter 2

Old Testament thought:
Deep within them I will plant my law,
writing it on their hearts.
I will forgive their iniquity
and never call their sin to mind.   (Jeremiah 31.33–4)

Vocal prayer:
    This is the day that the Lord has made,
    we will rejoice and be glad.
Give thanks to the Lord for he is good,
for his love has no end.
Let the sons of Israel say:
'His love has no end'.
The Lord's right hand has triumphed;
his right hand raised me up.
I shall not die, I shall live
and recount his deeds.
    This is the day that the Lord has made,
    I will rejoice and be glad. (From Psalm 118)

Gospel: John 20.19–21

ABC. On the evening of the day of his resurrection Jesus visited the disciples in the Upper Room. They were filled with joy on hearing his twice-repeated greeting: 'Peace be with you'. He commissioned them to continue or fill out the work he had accomplished by his passion and rising from the dead; to enable them to perform the task, he breathed the Holy Spirit upon them.

This is a commentary on the flowing of blood and water from the side of Christ on the cross. Inseparable from the paschal mystery was the birth of the Church, the true Body of Christ, flesh of his flesh and bone of his bone; whoever was touched by the Church would be touched by Christ.

As our Lord gave this commission and the gift of his own Spirit to the disciples he indicated what the effect of their healing touch was to be: the forgiveness of sins. 'Those whose sins you forgive, they are forgiven ...' The goal of his Church was to be the same goal as his had been on the cross: the overthrowing of the power of Satan. The peace that he gave them and which they were expected to hand on to the whole world was the peace of a healed conscience, the bringing of human hearts into line with the heart and mind of God. This peace, established and nourished through union with the Body of Christ, is the foundation of the kingdom of God. To extend that kingdom is the specific work of the Church.

Eight days later, again in the Upper Room, the Lord visited the disciples. The Church thereafter was quick to establish the custom of seeking the Lord's presence with them in the weekly celebration of the eucharist on the day of his resurrection. Thomas, absent on Easter Sunday, refused to believe that the Lord had risen, but now, present at the second visit and identifying him by his wounds, he proclaimed his faith: 'My Lord and my God'. We should not blame Thomas, for he was right in thinking that the qualification for being an apostle was to have been an eyewitness of the resurrection. None the less perhaps he already had sufficient evidence for belief. He knew of the empty tomb and this was the critical fact. The Lord said to Thomas: 'Happy are those who have not seen and yet believe.' May not the evangelist John have had in mind his own dawning of belief when, entering the tomb after Peter and seeing the grave clothes lying undisturbed but enclosing no corpse, 'he saw and he believed' (John 20.9). The resurrection appearances were a transitory phase in our Lord's revelation: his true home after rising from the dead was in the, for us, unimaginable dimension of heaven.

Easter 3

Old Testament thought:
They who eat me will hunger for more,
they who drink me will thirst for more.
Whoever listens to me will never have to blush,
whoever acts as I dictate will never sin.

(Ecclesiasticus 24.21–2)

Vocal prayer:
I will bless the Lord who gives me counsel,

who even at night directs my heart.

I keep the Lord ever in my sight:

since he is at my right hand, I shall stand firm.

And so my heart rejoices, my soul is glad;

even my body shall rest in safety.

For you will not leave my soul among the dead,

nor let your beloved know decay.

You will show me the path of life,

the fullness of joy in your presence,

at your right hand happiness for ever.

(From Psalm 16)

Gospel: Year A: Luke 24.13–35; *Year B:* Luke 24.35–48;
Year C: John 21.1–14

A. The meeting of two disciples with Jesus on the road to
Emmaus illustrates the fact that the forty days during
which our Lord appeared to the disciples after his resurrection was a period of transition. He appeared to them
and yet their recognition of him was hesitant. On this
occasion they did not recognize him at all. How could
they, for the eye of mortal man cannot yet look upon the
Lord as he really is.

And so as Jesus walked with those two disciples on their
way home, disconsolate now that the hope of deliverance
for Israel was shattered, they heard all he was saying and
were moved by his words, but they did not know that it
was Jesus speaking to them. They did, however, begin to
grasp the mystery of who the Messiah was – one who had
to suffer in order to inaugurate his kingdom – and what
the nature of his kingdom was – a kingdom not of this
world, but the rule of God in the hearts of men and
women.

Hoping, no doubt, to be further enlightened, they
invited Jesus to stay with them. And now comes the most
important revelation contained in this passage of Scripture. Jesus, asked as honoured guest to bless the meal,
broke the bread, and instantly they recognized who he
was, but only in the very moment that they could no
longer see him. They learned, as we must learn, that the
Lord's real presence with his Church is no longer to be
seen with the eye of the body, but with the eye of faith in
the bread and wine of the eucharist. The whole episode,
too, is a kind of symbol of the eucharist: the instruction
Jesus gave as they walked along the road when he
expounded the scriptures to them, explaining how the
Old Testament pointed towards himself, represents the
Liturgy of the Word, and the breaking of bread at the end
represents the Liturgy of the Upper Room.

B. The Gospel reading for this year has similarities with the Gospel of St John, read on Sunday Easter 2, and the commentary supplied for Year A is appropriate to this passage also, especially in respect of the stress at the end upon the Church's task of preaching repentance for forgiveness of sins.

This portion of St Luke's Gospel continues the theme of the road to Emmaus narrative in that it is a cryptic allusion to the eucharist. Jesus makes the puzzling request that they give him something to eat. How could he require bodily food as he now existed in a transfigured state? We find a clue in the story of Tobias where the angel, disclosing who he really is, says: 'You thought you saw me eating, but that was appearance and no more' (Tobit 12.19). All of the resurrection appearances suggest that Jesus was there and yet not there, for he was communicating with them from a world that was totally different from the one in which they lived. But some communication was needed, for they still required instruction.

Another clue is given us in the nature of the food they provided – fish. At the feeding of the multitude with the bread that foreshadowed the Bread of Life, there had also been some fish. The separate letters of the Greek word for 'fish' (I-CH-TH-U-S) supply the initials in Greek for 'Jesus Christ, of God, the Son, Saviour'. Fish is thus a code for our incarnate Lord. Luke tells us pointedly that Jesus ate the fish before their eyes: 'Look, do you understand what I am doing?' He was feeding upon his own substance, not upon bodily food at all. This scene, like the Emmaus scene, is a declaration that it is in the celebration of the eucharist that we are to seek the real presence of our Lord.

C. In this year the Gospel comes from the Epilogue of St John's Gospel. There are only seven apostles present. Seven is the universal number, unlike the number twelve which points to the twelve tribes of Israel, and here it tells us that the mission of the Church is to the whole world, not just to the people of the Old Covenant.

The seven have gone fishing, but their night-long efforts have been in vain. Then they see someone at the lake side; it is Jesus but they do not recognize him, just as the two disciples on the Emmaus road had failed to recognize him. Jesus says to them: 'Throw your net out to starboard and you'll find something.' Throughout the night they had toiled fruitlessly, perhaps concerned only about their old trade; but now under the direction of the Lord their work becomes a sign of their apostolic commitment and is successful; not only do they pull in a fine catch but a catch of 153, thought by St Jerome to be the number of species of fish in the Mediterranean.

The apostles were destined to go out into the whole world and bring into the kingdom of Christ men and women from all nations. Having done this they were to share with them the heavenly nourishment that the Lord alone could provide. On the shore Jesus had a meal of bread and fish already prepared for them. The bread was himself – the Bread of Life – and, as in the Gospel for this Sunday in Year B, we have the sign of the fish which is the code in Greek (ICHTHUS) for 'Jesus Christ, Son of God, Saviour'.

Easter 4

Old Testament thought:
Tell me then, you whom my heart loves:
Where will you lead your flock to graze,
where will you rest it at noon?
That I may no more wander like a vagabond
beside the flocks of your companions.

(Song of Songs 1.7)

Vocal prayer:
The Lord is my shepherd;
there is nothing I shall want.
Fresh and green are the pastures
where he gives me repose.
Near restful waters he leads me,
to revive my drooping spirit.
He guides me along the right path;
he is true to his name.
If I should walk in the valley of darkness
no evil would I fear.
You are there with your crook and your staff;
with these you give me comfort.   (From Psalm 23)

Gospel: Year A: John 10.1–10; *Year B:* John 10.11–18; *Year C:* John 10.27–30

The parable read on Good Shepherd Sunday is complex and the liturgy presents it in three instalments. In Year A we are introduced to the flock, to their sheepfold with its gate and gate-keeper, to the genuine shepherd, and to false and malicious shepherds.

The genuine shepherd, who enters by the proper entrance, is recognized by the gate-keeper and by the sheep. Jesus had come to the house of Israel according to the plan of God the Father. The humble in Israel who had observed the Law and listened to the prophets recognized him as the one accredited by the Law and the prophets, and so were prepared to follow him out to green pastures.

The blind leaders of Israel, to whom Jesus was speaking (John 9.40–1) did not understand the parable, so he developed his theme, likening himself now to the gate of the sheepfold, through which the sheep may safely go in to find shelter or out to find pasture. Jesus is the only gate through which men and women have access to God the Father and to the truth that brings life.

The last few lines of this section of the parable speak of false shepherds who will destroy the sheep. In contrast to these are true shepherds, who are recognized by the sheep because they too approach the flock through the gate who is the Lord, that is, by his appointment. We think of our Lord's threefold command to Peter, recorded at the conclusion of St John's Gospel: 'Feed my sheep'. It is appropriate that the liturgy prefaces the Gospel today with the account of Peter's opening up the gate of the universal sheepfold by his first sermon on the day of Pentecost. In the Church thereafter genuine shepherds have been recognized by their apostolic lineage and their being in communion with Peter.

B. This year we read the central part of the complex Good Shepherd parable. In Israel – and in the Middle

East generally – kings described themselves as shepherds; but in Israel the king was supposed to be a shepherd whose primary concern was for his flock and not for his self-aggrandisement. Jesus is the perfect king whose care of his flock will go to the length of dying for them.

Jesus, the Good Shepherd, is joined to his flock by his knowledge of them; and they for their part know him. Knowing, in the biblical sense, means more than intellectual comprehension; it is a union of mind and heart and will. Moreover, Jesus knows his flock in the same way as his Father knows him, so that his loving knowledge of his flock is a sharing with them of the divine life of love that he enjoys with the Father – a union with the divine nature. This mutual knowledge between Christ and his flock generates unity amongst all who submit to his will. God the Father loves his Son because of his readiness to lay down his life for the world, and also because he gives life to his disciples through taking up life again after his resurrection and blessing mankind with that new life. In all of his task of shepherding, Jesus fulfils the plan of his heavenly Father.

C. The short Gospel reading for today rounds off the complex parable of the Good Shepherd. Jesus, the Good Shepherd, gives eternal life to those who listen to his voice and follow him. The truth, recognized in the teaching of Jesus, and obedience to it, opens the gates of eternal life to the believer. In listening to and following Jesus the believer finds security, and need have no fear that adversaries of the truth will ever separate him from the flock of Jesus; but he must persevere in listening and following.

The believer's security rests finally upon the providence of God the Father, who has given the believer into the care of his Son, who is one with the Father in divinity, in heart, and in mind. The sacrifice of the Son on the cross was a sign of the Father's love for mankind, and the Son's resurrection a sign of the Father's love for the Son. Jesus was preoccupied with love of God the Father; our faith and life must likewise be wholly centred upon the service and adoration of God the Father.

Easter 5

Old Testament thought:
I am like a vine putting out graceful shoots,
my blossoms bear the fruit of glory and wealth.
Approach me, you who desire me,
and take your fill of my fruits.

(Ecclesiasticus 24.17–20)

Vocal prayer:
God of hosts, bring us back;
let your face shine on us and we shall be saved.
You brought a vine out of Egypt;
to plant it you drove out the nations.
Before it you cleared the ground;
it took root and spread through the land.
The mountains were covered with its shadow,
the cedars of God with its boughs.
God of hosts, turn again, we implore,
look down from heaven and see.
Visit this vine and protect it,
the vine your right hand has planted.

(From Psalm 80)

Gospel: Year A: John 14.1–12; *Year B:* John 15.1–8; *Year C:* John 14.21–7

A. During the time between Easter and Pentecost the Church, through the liturgical readings, helps us to understand the mystery of our Lord's perpetual presence amongst his people. Before his passion he had referred to himself as 'this temple' which after its destruction was to be rebuilt in three days. In his individual life on earth he was the place of God's dwelling, his temple, and after his resurrection he continued to be that temple in his body, the Church. The great theme of the Gospel readings at this season is therefore the mystery of the oneness of the Father and the Son in the bond of the Holy Spirit, and the extension of that unity into the body of Christ that is the Church. On the fifth Sunday of Easter in particular all three of the Gospel readings are variations on that theme.

Today we find the apostles with Jesus at the Last Supper. They are becoming fearful at the prospect of their Lord's departure. He comforts them by saying that he will return to them, having prepared a place for them in his Father's house. His remark that in that house there are many mansions is often taken to be an indication that the world we know is far from being the whole of God's creation. This may be so, but our Lord's words have a more precise meaning. Jesus himself is the Father's house, the new temple of God amongst men. In that temple there will be room for all of the apostles and for those who through their preaching come to believe in the Lord. Thus, finding a place in the body of Christ who is the temple of God, the believer begins to share in the life of God the Father. The reply Jesus gave to Thomas follows immediately upon the statement about his Father's house. Jesus said that he was the Way to the Father. Living in the Father's house is the same as living in union with God the Father through his Son.

The passage concludes with the assertion that the

Church will have the ability to continue the same redemptive work that Jesus had performed upon earth.

B. The Gospel for this Sunday vividly describes the mystery of the Church – its physical union with Christ the Lord, a union as real as that which joins a vine-stock to the branches that it supports. The vine-stock is the incarnate Son of God, the branches the members of the Church; but let us note that another Person occupies an important place in the parable. The vine is tended by God the Father. He planted the vine and he prunes it.

The Father's pruning is however effected through the word that his Son has spoken to the disciples. In this statement there is an allusion to the unity between Father and Son; and it is this unity within the Trinity that engenders the union between disciples and God the Father through Jesus. The Church throughout its entire history has to be pruned by the teaching of Jesus, and it is only in the measure that disciples remain true to the words of our Lord that their prayers will be effective. 'If you remain in me and my words remain in you, you may ask what you will and you shall get it.'

The purpose for which men and women have been brought into union with God the Father, drawing life from the incarnate Son who is the root of the vine, is to bear fruit that gives glory to God the Father. God the Father plants and tends the vine and finally rejoices in its fruit.

C. Meditation on the profound teaching of the Gospel for today may be assisted by reading the second lesson at Mass – Apocalypse 21.1–5. In his vision John saw the universe and mankind transfigured in perfect beauty and holiness. God himself was the agent of transfiguration: the tabernacle of God had descended from heaven to earth; the Word had become flesh and God now dwelt amongst men and women.

Love had come down from heaven, but a love that was

more than natural affection which can be capricious. It was the love that God the Father has for God the Son, and the Son for the Father, a love that manifested itself in the obedience which moved the Son to offer himself in the sacrifice that was necessary for the accomplishment of the Father's desire that mankind be redeemed, so that the mutual love of Father and Son become manifest in an outpouring of love by men and women for each other. Again that love had to be love come down from heaven, a sharing in the love that dwells in the heart of the Blessed Trinity, a love that is totally self-giving. True love always carries a cross of some kind. Jesus said: 'Just as I have loved you, you also must love one another.'

Easter 6

Old Testament thought:
What great nation is there that has its gods so near as
  our God is to us?
And what great nation is there that has laws and customs
  to match this Law?   (Deuteronomy 4.7–8)

Vocal prayer:
Happy indeed is the man
who follows not the counsel of the wicked
nor lingers in the way of sinners
nor sits in the company of scorners;
but whose delight is in the law of the Lord
and who ponders his law day and night.
He is like a tree that is planted
beside the flowing waters;
that yields its fruit in due season
and whose leaves shall never fade;
and all that he does shall prosper.   (From Psalm 1)

Gospel: Year A: John 14.15–21; *Year B:* John 15.9–17; *Year C:* John 14.23–9

A. The Gospel for this Sunday in each year records our Lord's insistence on obedience to his commandments. Jesus links love with obedience, for to love someone is to desire and work for their good, and to know what is good we must understand the design according to which God has created all things. This design can be seen in his Word, imprinted in nature, and revealed in his law, in particular in the teaching of his Son.

So that his disciples would be capable of love founded upon knowledge and understanding, Jesus promised his disciples a share in his Spirit – the Spirit of truth. He will ask the Father to send another 'Advocate'. This translation of the Greek *parakletos* does not do justice to our Lord's meaning. Behind the Greek was the Hebrew concept of the *goel*, the nearest male relation of a man who had died. It was the duty of this man to assume the duties of the deceased husband and father. The Holy Spirit is thus our Lord's kinsman, who will comfort the orphaned disciples after the Lord's death.

Jesus concludes this part of his discourse by affirming his substantial union with God the Father, a union which he intends to share with his disciples, with his bride, the Church.

B. The Gospel-excerpt for today is the sequel to the parable of the vine, and the first sentence in today's reading sums up the teaching of that parable: 'As the Father has loved me, so I have loved you'. The root-stock and the whole vine, as well as the husbandman who tends the vine, are portrayed as a single entity; and so the stream of love that flows from the Father, who is the husbandman, through the Son, who is the stock, and up into all of the branches, who are the Church, is one and the same stream of divine love.

This sequel to the parable of the vine makes clear also

that mediation of the Father's love and Spirit to the Church comes through the sacrifice of the Son: 'A man can have no greater love than to lay down his life for his friends'.

The mystery of the unity of the Blessed Trinity and of the love that is the heart of the Trinity, determines the way in which Christians pray. It is by the enlightenment and power of the Holy Spirit that the Christian is able to pray; but that Spirit is no isolated deity, for he has come to the Church from the side of Christ on the cross; and the prayer thus initiated is directed back through Christ the Son to God the Father, who is the ultimate source of love and to whom the fruits of all Christian endeavour give glory.

C. In the third year in the cycle the Gospel again contains our Lord's admonition to keep his commandments, and to link love with obedience. Speaking of the Spirit whom he is about to send, Jesus stresses the function of the Spirit as teacher of the truth that he had taught them. This is of supreme importance because if keeping his word and commandments is essential, if the love of God is to dwell in them, then they, and those to whom they convey the words of Christ, must be assured of the authenticity of their teaching.

Throughout the long discourse in the Upper Room Jesus had been preoccupied with the thought of his heavenly Father, with the bond of love that binds him to the Father, and with his longing to sacrifice himself so that mankind might be caught up within that same bond of love, which is the Holy Spirit. And so he tried to turn the disciples' minds away from himself and towards the Father. They ought not be afraid at the prospect of his leaving them; they would not be if their love for him was so perfect that they shared his confidence in the Father. He is going through death to the Father so that the Father's benign plan for their redemption can be accomplished. It is time they learned to imitate him in that love for the Father which would enable him to say on the Cross: 'Father, into your hands I commend my spirit'.

'If you loved me you would have been glad to know that I am going to the Father, for the Father is greater than I' (John 14.28)

The Ascension of the Lord

Old Testament thought:
The Lord encircles his people
now and for always.   (From Psalm 125)

Vocal prayer:
   Alleluia!
God goes up with shouts of joy;
the Lord goes up with trumpet blast.
Sing praise for God, sing praise,
sing praise to our king, sing praise.
   Alleluia!
God is king of all the earth.
Sing praise with all your skill.
God is king over the nations;
God reigns on his holy throne.
   Alleluia!   (From Psalm 47)

Gospel: Year A: Matthew 28.16–20; *Year B:* Mark 16.15–20; *Year C:* Luke 24.46–53

ABC. With slight variation in detail Matthew, Mark and Luke tell of the risen Lord's farewell to the apostles.

The last two sentences of Matthew's account are important; they record our Lord's command to the apostles to baptize believers in the name of the Father and of the Son and of the Holy Spirit, so that they might become incorporated into the life and love of the Blessed Trinity; then the mandate continues: 'Teach them to observe all the commands I gave you. And know that I am with you always; yes, to the end of time'. As in the discourse at the Last Supper, so again in the last sentence he spoke to his apostles, Jesus linked love with obedience. True love is a sharing in the life of God, mediated through the sacrament of baptism, and so it must also be a sharing in his will, made known to us in his commandments.

Our Lord's ascension into heaven is the last of his resurrection appearances. All of these appearances resembled the ascension, for they all ended with his vanishing from their sight. The spell of forty days between the resurrection and the ascension was a period of transition, made necessary on account of the disciples' inability immediately to understand the meaning of all that had happened. They still needed some instruction – a commentary on the paschal mystery. In the book of Acts St Luke makes that very point, 'for forty days he had continued to appear to them and tell them about the kingdom of God'.

The resurrection appearances were a means of communication between two quite different worlds – the world of bodily life and the heavenly world of eternal life. There was never meant to be any permanent reality about the Lord's communicating with the apostles in this world after his resurrection. These were, strictly speaking, appearances. St Luke's observation, that at the meal in Emmaus the two disciples recognized Jesus only at the moment of his vanishing from their bodily sight, is most significant. The Lord's presence in reality was henceforth to be found in the eucharist.

———————————————

Easter 7

Old Testament thought:
To acknowledge you is indeed the perfect virtue,
to know your power is the root of immortality.

(Wisdom 15.3)

Vocal prayer:
The Lord is my light and my help;
whom shall I fear?
The Lord is the stronghold of my life;
before whom shall I shrink?
There is one thing I ask of the Lord,
for this I long,
to live in the house of the Lord,
all the days of my life,
to savour the sweetness of the Lord,
to behold his temple.
O Lord, hear my voice when I call;
have mercy and answer.
Of you my heart has spoken:
'Seek his face.'

(From Psalm 27)

Gospel: Year A: John 17.1–11; *Year B:* John 17.11–19; *Year C:* John 17.20–6

A. Having finished his discourse to the apostles in the Upper Room, Jesus moved into his priestly prayer in which he looks forward to the climax of his life in the 'Hour' when he will decisively glorify his Father by an act of perfect sacrifice. He prays that in this act he too will be glorified; this mutual glorifying will be the sign of the perfect unity of love between Father and Son.

The Son sacrifices himself and rises from the dead in his human nature, and so in the Son human nature is taken up into the life of God. The disciples by faith recognize the oneness of Father and Son, and in this knowledge find eternal life, for eternal life is to know the Father through the Son. In this knowledge men and women are caught up in the Holy Spirit, that is, into the bond of love that unites Father and Son.

While the final glorification of the Son is deferred until the end of time, the glory of God is now seen in the world in the Body of Christ, the Church, which is the embryo of his eternal kingdom. Jesus said: 'I am not in the world any longer, but they are in the world, keep those you have given me true to your name, so that they may be one like us.' To be 'one like us' and to be 'true to your name' is to share in the power of God's life which is love, so that, in his Church, our Lord Jesus can be truly in the world.

B. In this year we continue to read from our Lord's priestly prayer, spoken on the eve of his Passion. In this he declared the purpose of his life, death and resurrection. It was to call disciples and save them from the power of evil and death by giving them a share in the fulness of life, the life which he shared with his heavenly Father. He would accomplish this by offering himself in death, trusting in the Father's power to raise him from the dead. Three concepts dominate this part of the priestly prayer: unity, joy, truth.

Unity is not an external formality; it is the devotion to one another of persons. The Son's devotion to the Father is complete, the product of perfect identity of mind, heart, and will; and the disciples of Jesus are drawn into this life of reciprocal devotion and knowledge. This sharing of divine life maintains unity within the community of disciples.

The *joy* which sharing in this life brings is no mere effervescent euphoria, but deep tranquillity, peace that wells up from the stream of a secure and fulfilled life.

Truth is grasped through hearing and obeying God's word. Jesus had consecrated himself to the truth, and in this prayer he reveals that he did so in order that his disciples likewise would be consecrated in truth. Thus we come back to a fundamental theme in our Lord's teaching: the gifts of joy, peace, unity, and holiness derive from knowledge of God, who is truth.

C. In the third year of the cycle we read the conclusion of our Lord's priestly prayer. Earlier in this prayer he had said, 'I am not praying for the world but for those you have given me.' Now at the end of his prayer he does pray for the world. 'I pray not only for these, but for those also who through their words will believe in me'. He prays further that through their belief the world too may come to share in that oneness which he enjoys with the Father and into which he had drawn the apostles. By praying first of all for the original disciples, the apostles in particular, our Lord stressed the fact that there is a distinction between the Church and the world. The Church needs his special prayer and concern so that it may be true to its mission.

But our Lord did not mean the division between Church and world to be permanent. While the Church will always be distinct from the world, the mission of the Church is to expand by drawing into that perfect unity as much of the world as possible; and the authenticity of the Church will be accredited by her unity. 'May they all be one. Father, may they be one in us, as you are in me and I in you, so that the world may believe it was you who sent me.' That perfect unity is not however a quality given directly to the world, but a supernatural gift given to the Church and then indirectly to those who become assimilated into her divine life. God's ultimate plan is that world should become Church – the Bride of Christ.

Pentecost

Old Testament thought:
a. Throughout the earth men spoke the same language. They said, 'Let us build a tower with its top reaching heaven. Let us make a name for ourselves.' The Lord confused the language of the whole earth.

(From Genesis 11)

b. The Lord called to Moses, 'These are the words you are to speak to the sons of Israel.'

(From Exodus 19)

c. I shall put my spirit in you, and you will live.

(Ezekiel 37.14)

Vocal prayer:
Bless the Lord, my soul!
Lord God, how great you are,
clothed in majesty and glory,
wrapped in light as in a robe!
How many are your works, O Lord!
In wisdom you have made them all.
The earth is full of your riches.
You take back your spirit, they die,
returning to the dust from which they came.
You send forth your spirit, they are created;
and you renew the face of the earth.

(From Psalm 104)

Gospel: John 20.19–23

To meditate profitably upon Pentecost – the completion of the paschal mystery – we must understand how it is the fulfilment of several strands of Old Testament thought. It may be best to separate three strands in this meditation.

a. In the beginning, that is in God's creative design, the human race was one over the whole earth, and this unity, this spiritual harmony was symbolized by its having but a single language. Pride and arrogance, directed first towards the Creator himself, and then overflowing into conflict between men and women, is portrayed in the Bible by the story of the Tower of Babel, a mighty ziggurat such as one could see in Ur of Chaldea. The biblical writer saw such terraced temples as expressions of mankind's attempt to reach the heights of heaven by its own power. To confound men and women in their arrogance the Lord punished them by creating many languages, a sign of their inability to live in harmony.

On Pentecost Sunday we read the account of the gift of tongues to enable the apostles to communicate with all nations. It was not for this purpose alone, however, that the gift was given: it signified also the abrogation of the curse of Babel; mankind was having its primeval unity and harmony of spirit restored through the paschal mystery of Christ.

b. Moses ascended the mountain of the Lord and brought down for the people the truth in the Ten Commandments. Pentecost was an ancient harvest festival, which the Israelites had adapted as a commemoration of the giving of the Law through Moses. The Lord Jesus, having ascended into the presence of God the Father, returned in his Spirit to the people to proclaim the new Law, the fullness of truth. The festival of Pentecost was an appropriate time on which to do this. The Christian Pentecost is thus the festival in celebration of the new law, of the new and everlasting covenant God has made with his people. Our Lord not only inaugurated the new Law on the Day of Pentecost, but at the same time empowered his apostles to be reliable preachers of his new law, of his eternal truth, and to be the effective administrators of the sacraments associated with it.

When the prophet Jeremiah had foretold the giving of the Spirit of God to all mankind he spoke of the new mode in which the Law of God would be given. He said: 'Deep within them I will plant my Law, writing it in their hearts.' The Spirit that now came through the paschal mystery of Christ was no mere knowledge of God's Law, but knowledge allied with love of that Law. God's Law was no longer to be felt as a restraint, something to be obeyed but chafed against, or to be obeyed in a spirit of self-righteousness in the hope of gaining merit, of becoming God's creator, for the Spirit of Christ would bind men and women to the mind and will of God the Father in joy and love. They would see the commandments of God as a revelation of his love, so that keeping his laws they would only be benefiting themselves. Long ago King Solomon had prayed to be given a *heart* to discern between good and evil. Even in Old Testament times devout men and women knew that their need was not only to know God's law, but to learn to love it. At last on the Day of Pentecost, The Holy Spirit had come through Christ to satisfy the deepest needs of all men and women.

c. The Gospel reading for Pentecost Sunday takes us back to the first Easter Day, which reminds us that Pentecost, the coming of the Holy Spirit, is the final act in the paschal drama. The outpouring of the Spirit at Pentecost was not a new redemptive act, unrelated to the events of Easter, but its final manifestation. The giving of the Holy Spirit is the fruit of the glorification of Christ on the cross. 'Into your hands I commend my Spirit', our Lord said, but his giving up the Spirit through death was for the sake of mankind. And so on the evening of the day of his resurrection Jesus manifested himself to the disciples and said: 'Receive the Holy Spirit'. Peace, the indwelling of the Spirit, and the power to reconcile men and women with God and with each other – are the three realities which together make up the fruit of the paschal mystery, and in the possession of these is the glorification of the Church, which our Lord said would be joined with his own glorification on the cross.

The restoration of true love to the heart of mankind is what the indwelling of the Holy Spirit accomplishes. The Pentecost liturgy reminds us that this indwelling was already effected at Easter. At Pentecost the Spirit then gave power to the apostles, and through them to all members of the Church, to carry out their specific functions and to evangelize the world, but all of these particular gifts would be useless did they not flow from the fundamental charism of unity and love, which flows from the side of Christ on the cross.

Trinity Sunday (First Sunday After Pentecost)

Old Testament thought:
I, Wisdom, was by his side, a master craftsman,
delighting him day after day,
at play everywhere in his world,
delighting to be with the sons of men.

(Proverbs 8.30–1)

Vocal prayer:
You are blest, Lord God of our fathers
To you glory and praise for evermore.
Blest your glorious holy name.
To you glory and praise for evermore.
You are blest in the temple of your glory.
To you glory and praise for evermore.
You are blest on the throne of your kingdom.
To you glory and praise for evermore.
You are blest who gaze into the depths.
To you glory and praise for evermore.
You are blest in the firmament of heaven.
To you glory and praise for evermore.

(From Daniel 3)

Gospel: Year A: John 3.16–18; *Year B:* Matthew 28.16–20; *Year C:* John 16.12–15

ABC. Over a period of roughly six months at Sunday Mass the Liturgy of the Word has told the story of mankind's redemption. This was presented in two phases: 1. from Advent until the feast of the Baptism of our Lord; 2. from Lent until Pentecost. The conclusion of that great drama having been reached, we are now urged to relax and enjoy the end to which the redemption of mankind was directed: the perfect adoration of almighty God, and mankind's enjoyment of his fellowship for all eternity. The Old Testament reading at Mass in Year A describes how Moses, having reached the summit of mount Sinai, 'bowed down to the ground at once and worshipped him'.

Today the liturgy presents us therefore with texts that speak of the nature of God. We are invited to turn our minds and hearts to contemplation of the mystery of the Blessed Trinity. The Gospels assigned to the Sundays in the three-year cycle all proclaim that the one God is a Trinity of three Persons – Father, Son, and Holy Spirit. St John, by emphasizing the Father's love in sending his Son, so that mankind could be brought back into his friendship and share in his love, makes it clear that the Spirit of truth is indeed holy, the personification no less than the love that binds God the Father with God the Son. The Holy Spirit is love itself.

We must not therefore think of the mystery of the Blessed Trinity as an intellectual conundrum, an arithmetical puzzle. It is about the mystery of love. Love exists between persons. If the eternal and self-subsistent God is love he must in some way love himself from all eternity, for before the creation he alone existed. Within the Godhead there is an act of eternal loving. God the Father loves his Son, and the love that is thus engendered is itself a divine Person – the Holy Spirit of love.

And that is not all. The mystery of the Trinity overflows into the mystery of mankind's redemption. As a result of the perfect sacrifice of his incarnate Son, God the Father has welcomed men and women back into his friendship; through his Son's dying and rising he has poured out the Holy Spirit of love upon human flesh and so shared divine life with mankind. 'In making these gifts he has given us the guarantee of something very great and wonderful to come: through them you will be able to share the divine nature' (2 Peter 1.4).

The Body and Blood of Christ (Second Sunday after Pentecost)

Old Testament thought:
He gives him honey from the rock to taste,
and oil from the flinty crag,
rich food of the wheat's ear,
and blood of the fermenting grape for drink.
(Deuteronomy 32.13–14)

Vocal prayer:
How can I repay the Lord
for his goodness to me?
The cup of salvation I will raise;
I will call on the Lord's name.
O precious in the eyes of the Lord
is the death of his faithful.
Your servant, Lord, your servant am I;
you have loosened my bonds.
A thanksgiving sacrifice I make:
I will call on the Lord's name.
My vows to the Lord I will fulfil
before all his people.
(From Psalm 116)

Gospel: Year A: John 6.51–8; *Year B:* Mark 14.12–16, 22–6; *Year C:* Luke 9.11–17

ABC. St John provides a commentary on the miracle of the feeding with loaves and fishes, which he saw as a foreshadowing of the eucharist; St Mark recounts the institution of the eucharist; St Luke describes the miraculous feeding of the multitude with five loaves and two fish. Any one of these readings, or all of them together, can be used as a foundation for meditation on the mystery of the eucharist.

To assist our meditation now we could read the comments made on the readings in Holy Week, for this feast is in a sense a repetition during the year of the celebration of the mystery of the Hour of Jesus, as indeed is the celebration of every eucharist; or we could simply recall some basic facts.

In John chapter 6 Jesus speaks both of his sacrifice on the cross – 'the bread that I shall give is my flesh, for the life of the world' – and of the eating of that bread sacramentally in the eucharist – 'anyone who eats this bread will live for ever'. The cross and the eucharist are the key to understanding what Jesus said after he had fed the multitude, although at the time neither the crowd nor the disciples knew of these later events; but we can learn from that episode that there is an identity between the sacrifice of the cross and the sacramental eating of the eucharist. The eucharist is a meal and also a sacrifice – the sacrifice of the cross.

Something else that Jesus said after the miraculous feeding is supremely important. When many people turned away from him because of his 'hard saying', his 'intolerable language', about eating his flesh and drinking his blood, he explained to the Twelve: 'What if you should see the Son of Man ascend to where he was before? It is the spirit that gives life'. Eating his flesh has to be understood spiritually, which does not mean 'symbolically', but that the flesh eaten in the eucharist is not the finite flesh of Jesus as it was when he hung upon the cross, but that flesh glorified in his resurrection by the power of the Holy Spirit. It was the identical Person who rose, but his flesh had been transfigured and acquired new properties.

It is the substance of this glorified body that is truly present in the bread and wine of the eucharist, and is the food which, as we feed upon it week by week or day by day, will progressively 'transfigure these wretched bodies of ours into copies of his glorious body' (Philippians 4.21).

Sundays in Ordinary time, Cycle A

Sunday 2(A)

Old Testament thought:
I will make you the light of the nations
so that my salvation may reach to the ends of the earth.

(Isaiah 49.6)

Vocal prayer:

Here I am, Lord!

I come to do your will.

I waited, I waited for the Lord

and he stooped down to me,

he heard my cry.

He put a new song in my mouth,

praise of our God.

Here I am, Lord!

I come to do your will.

(From Psalm 40)

Gospel: John 1.29–34

On the second Sunday in ordinary time the Epiphany theme is continued – the true identity of Jesus of Nazareth is being proclaimed. In the incident we read today John the Baptist is the agent of that proclamation. John pointed to Jesus and made three fundamental statements about him.

1. He announced that Jesus was the Lamb of God, thus identifying him with the Suffering Servant of the Lord, whose coming had been prophesied by Isaiah, and whose mission was to remove sin from the world. 2. He declared that Jesus had existed before him. In John 8.58 this affirmation is made by Jesus himself: 'Before Abraham ever was, I Am.' He existed before the creation: he is the Wisdom of God. 3. He reported that he had seen the Holy Spirit descending on Jesus like a dove, and resting on him: Jesus was the Messiah, the 'Anointed One'. At the very beginning of our Lord's public activity John had made it clear that the Messiah and the Suffering Servant are one. Throughout his life Jesus was to stress this fact frequently.

As well as making these statements John explained, 'I did not know him myself', meaning that he had recognized who Jesus really was, not by his own wisdom but through divine inspiration. He had been assured that the descent of the Spirit upon Jesus would be the sign that this man was truly the Messiah.

The divine revelation to John the Baptist concludes by announcing the new baptism that Jesus will institute. Jesus, the incarnate Son of God, had been anointed in this way not for his own sake but so that he could, through his flesh, cause the Holy Spirit to rest upon all men and women.

Sunday 3(A)

Old Testament thought:
The people that walked in darkness
has seen a great light;
on those who live in a land of deep shadow
a light has shined.   (Isaiah 9.1)

Vocal prayer:
The Lord is my light and my help;
whom shall I fear?
The Lord is the stronghold of my life;
before whom shall I shrink?
There is one thing I ask of the Lord,
for this I long,
to live in the house of the Lord,
all the days of my life,
to savour the sweetness of the Lord,
to behold his temple.
I am sure that I shall see the Lord's goodness
in the land of the living.
Hope in him, hold firm and take heart.
Hope in the Lord!   (From Psalm 27)

Gospel: Matthew 4.12–23

After his baptism in the Jordan river and his subsequent temptations in the wilderness, Jesus set off to inaugurate his kingdom or rule. His mission overlapped in some degree with that of John the Baptist, for he continued to call people to repentance; but he also promised men and women new life and enlightenment. It had been expected that the Messiah would appear first in Judea, but Jesus chose to return to his native Galilee, first because John's arrest warned him to steer clear of Herod for the time being, and second because the prophet Isaiah had foretold that the light extinguished in the northern kingdom when that province was annexed to Assyria in 721 BC would be rekindled in the Messianic age.

Without the light of Christ's teaching we would all flounder in moral darkness. Do we make every effort to become enlightened by our Lord – through study of the Scriptures and of the teaching of the Church, and through prayer and the use of the sacraments?

Our Lord's first act was to call the apostles, to ensure that there would for ever be competent witnesses to him and his teaching. But the Twelve and their successors are not the only witnesses to Christ. All believers have a sacrificial and prophetic calling. The Faith is to be kept but also to be given on to others. The Church is not a cosy club of like-minded people, enjoying the comfort of religious experience, but a living body ready to make sacrifices for the redemption of the whole world.

Sunday 4(A)

Old Testament thought:
In your midst I will leave
a humble and lowly people.   (Zephaniah 3.12)

Vocal prayer:
It is the Lord who keeps faith for ever,
who is just to those who are oppressed.
It is he who gives bread to the hungry,
the Lord, who sets prisoners free.
It is the Lord who gives sight to the blind,
who raises up those who are bowed down,
the Lord, who protects the stranger
and upholds the widow and orphan.
It is the Lord, who loves the just
but thwarts the path of the wicked.
the Lord will reign for ever,
Zion's God, from age to age.   (From Psalm 146)

Gospel: Matthew 5.1–12

The Mountain: In St Matthew's Gospel the mountain symbolizes the place of God's action and revelation. In the background we have to imagine Mount Sinai, where the Law was first given. In his Sermon on the Mount Jesus set out the ground rules of his kingdom. He did not give us a fully worked-out moral teaching – that is for his Church to do under the guidance of the Holy Spirit – but described in nine promises of blessedness, the fundamental disposition of mind and heart which must characterize his disciples.

The poor in spirit: This poverty is often, but not always, linked with material poverty. Its essence is the spiritual childhood necessary for entry into God's kingdom. The poor in spirit are unconditionally obedient to God's law, and firm in their trust in God's care and ultimate vindication of righteousness. There is therefore an eschatological dimension to this poverty, for it looks to the heavenly realization of God's kingdom. The rewards promised to the disciple are to come in that future kingdom but the blessedness, which is the real reward, is given here and now. The person who is able to show perfect obedience to, and total trust in, God enjoys the peace of Christ which is the crown of all blessedness.

The kingdom of God: The Jerusalem Bible provides this note: 'The sovereignty of God over the Chosen People, and through them over the world, is at the heart of Christ's preaching ... It implies a kingdom of "saints" where God will be truly King because they will acknowledge his royal rights by knowing and loving him.' The kingdom of God, entered through poverty, which is equated with spiritual childhood, is within us.

Sunday 5(A)

Old Testament thought:
Share your bread with the hungry,
and shelter the homeless poor,
clothe the man you see to be naked
and turn not from your own kin.
Then will your light shine like the dawn
and your wound be quickly healed over.   (Isaiah 58.7–8)

Vocal prayer:
Lord, who shall dwell on your holy mountain?
He who walks without fault;
he who acts with justice
and speaks the truth from his heart;
he who does not slander with his tongue.
He who does no wrong to his brother,
who casts no slur on his neighbour,
who holds the godless in disdain,
but honours those who fear the Lord.
He who keeps his pledge, come what may;
who takes no interest on a loan
and accepts no bribes against the innocent.
Such a man will stand firm for ever.   (Psalm 15)

Gospel: Matthew 5.13–16

The images of salt and of light are pre-eminently applicable to our Lord Jesus himself, for he is the Light of the world, and he is the salt that preserves mankind for eternal life and imparts savour to life on earth.

In the parables we read in this Gospel passage, Jesus applied these images to his Church. He grants therefore to his Mystical Body as a whole, and to every believer, the privilege of sharing in his vocation. The Church is to be like salt, like a city on a hill-top, and like a lamp in a dark room.

It is our duty to radiate joy in our own lives and so bring happiness to all around us. We must be like a city built on a hill-top – as so many little cities in the Mediterranean region are – the sight of which, especially as night is drawing on and the city's lights are seen, welcomes the weary traveller with the prospect of food and a place to sleep for the night. This image applies particularly to the Church as a family in which men and women can find a true home. The image of the lamp in a room is a variation on the city image, speaking of the happiness of a family who, when the lamp is lit, gather round to enjoy one another's company.

The Church raises up the heart of society like leaven in a loaf, but the Christian is not merely a 'do-gooder'; he is an evangelist who leads others to God: 'Let your light so shine, that they may see your good works *and give glory to your Father who is in heaven*'.

Sunday 6(A)

Old Testament thought:
God, create a clean heart in me,
put into me a new and constant spirit.   (Psalm 51.10)

Vocal prayer:
Happy indeed is the man
who follows not the counsel of the wicked,
but who delights in the law of the Lord.
He is like a tree that is planted
beside the flowing waters,
that yields its fruit in due season.   (From Psalm 1)

Gospel: Matthew 5.17–37

First, Jesus explained the relationship of his law to the Old Testament law. The old law, he affirmed, must be observed in every detail until a certain point in time when all that the law and the prophets foretold will have been *fulfilled*. When did that *fulfilment* come? With the death and resurrection of Jesus. At that point the new age arrived, and from then on Christians became bound by the commands of Jesus, whether or not these agreed with the old law.

In the following six antitheses ('You have heard it said ... but I say') Jesus gave six examples of corrections of the old law. We notice, however, that he upheld and reinforced the core of the old law, the Ten Commandments, by pointing out that external observance was not enough: one had to love the law, and become purified in mind and heart and will. It was the derivative laws, especially the many ritual precepts, and the intepretations of the law that he corrected.

A good example is his prohibition of divorce. He revoked the Mosaic permission of divorce, and the exception to his own rule is only apparent. 'Except on the grounds of adultery' does not mean that divorce is permissible if a wife has committed adultery, but that if a couple are living in an incestuous union that union may, indeed must, be discontinued. Jesus was thus condemning divorce absolutely. He also condemned the use of oaths, which were prescribed by the old law.

Sunday 7(A)

Old Testament thought:
You must not bear hatred for your brother in your heart.
(Leviticus 19.17)

Vocal prayer:
The Lord is compassion and love.
My soul give thanks to the Lord,
all my being, bless his holy name.
My soul, give thanks to the Lord
and never forget all his blessings.
It is he who forgives all your guilt,
who heals every one of your ills,
who redeems your life from the grave,
who crowns you with love and compassion.
The Lord is compassion and love,
slow to anger and rich in mercy.
He does not treat us according to our sins
nor repay us according to our faults.
The Lord is compassion and love.   (From Psalm 103)

Gospel: Matthew 5.38–48

The Sermon on the Mount continues by describing confrontational situations, wherein the disciple of Jesus must act or react in a way that is quite contrary to the way of the world. People write off Jesus' demands, saying that they are totally unrealistic. They may well be, but only if we fall into the trap of rigidly literal interpretation.

In these precepts Jesus is not setting out a set of rules of action that can be slavishly copied. He is shocking us out of our complacency, which encourages us always to adopt as a first principle of conduct, that no one is ever going to take advantage of me and get away with it. For example, if I am insulted – which is what the blow by the back of the hand signifies – my spontaneous response is to fly into a rage, to return insults and even to take revenge. By telling us that we ought to be ready to suffer a further blow, Jesus is pointing out that our actions and reactions should be motivated by the desire to reach reconciliation with everyone. The question of how we ought to maintain justice in society, protect innocent victims, and restrain evildoers, is not the question Jesus is dealing with here. The whole thrust of the Sermon on the Mount is to urge us to acquire a perfect heart, a heart that reflects the infinite patience and compassion of God.

Sunday 8(A)

Old Testament thought:
Does a woman forget her baby at the breast,
or fail to cherish the son of her womb?
Yet even if these forget,
I will never forget you.   (Isaiah 49.15)

Vocal prayer:
In God alone is my soul at rest;
my help comes form him.
He alone is my rock, my stronghold,
my fortress: I stand firm.
In God is my safety and glory,
the rock of my strength.
Take refuge in God all you people.
Trust him at all times.
Pour out your hearts before him.   (From Psalm 62)

Gospel: Matthew 6.24–34

As he came to the end of his Sermon on the Mount Jesus adopted a looser style of teaching, while at the same time focusing attention on fundamental ideas. The Beatitudes with which his discourse had begun illumined the dispositions which should direct all the actions of his disciples; now in conclusion Jesus elucidated the disposition which embraced all the rest.

One principle ought to govern the life of every disciple: 'Set your hearts on God's kingdom first and all else will be given you.' The disciple of Christ is to be distinguished from others by single-minded worship and service of God, the opposite of which is preoccupation with mammon – an Aramaic word that means 'property'.

Jesus began this section of his teaching with the firm statement that the worship of God and the worship of wordly possessions are mutually exclusive. There can be no compromise here. One may be inclined to ask whether this does not commit the disciple to irresponsibility concerning the management of earthly affairs. Our Lord was very careful in the way he worded his command. He said: 'Seek *first* the things of the kingdom.' If one does this, then he will be able to arrange his wordly affairs sensibly. It is a question of priority. The disciple pays proper attention to his earthly duties – providing for himself and his family – but never becomes absorbed in these things.

There is more to our Lord's teaching on this topic. The single-minded devotion the disciple shows towards God our heavenly Father expresses also awareness of the Father's perfect love of mankind, and so is a form of trust in his providence. This trust does not encourage irresponsibility or laziness over mundane duties, but drives out all anxiety, so that even the management of earthly concerns becomes a way of working for the advancement of the kingdom of heaven.

Sunday 9(A)

Old Testament thought:
Moses said to the people:
'See, I set before you today a blessing and a curse:
a blessing, if you obey the commands of the Lord;
a curse, if you disobey the commandments of the Lord.'
(Deuteronomy 11.26–8)

Vocal prayer:
Happy indeed is the man
who follows not the counsel of the wicked
nor lingers in the way of sinners
nor sits in the company of scorners;
but whose delight is the law of the Lord
and who ponders his law day and night.
He is like a tree that is planted
beside the flowing waters,
that yields its fruit in due season
and whose leaves shall never fade;
and all that he does shall prosper.
Not so are the wicked, not so.   (From Psalm 1)

Gospel: Matthew 7.21–7

The Sermon on the Mount had begun in antithetical style, blessings being contrasted with woes; the Sermon ends in the same style: the narrow gate is contrasted with the wide gate; false prophets – those who make a great show of calling out to the Lord in ecstasy – with true prophets; and finally, in today's reading, the house built on rock with the house built on sand. In each case the contrast is between those who pay lip-service to our Lord's teaching and those who act upon his teaching.

In the climax of his great discourse preached on the mountain, Jesus aimed criticism at the sin which besets religious people especially. He was warning all would-be disciples to beware of enjoying the outward forms of religion or of trying – without perhaps realizing it – to acquire power or prestige as leaders in the Church, whereas they ought to direct all their desire towards obeying his commands in humility and loving gratitude. It would be disastrous to fall into this sin, as this concluding parable makes clear. The house fell – 'and what a fall it had'. The section of Matthew's Gospel which records the Sermon on the Mount ends with the observation that the people were amazed at his teaching. They were impressed not just by the teaching but by his authoritative manner. He had dared even to correct the Mosaic law: 'but I say to you'. They had been listening to the one who at the end of time would, if they disobeyed him, pronounce judgement on them.

Sunday 10(A)

Old Testament thought:
What I want is love, not sacrifice;
knowledge of God, not holocausts.   (Hosea 6.6)

Vocal prayer:
A pure heart create for me, O God,
put a steadfast spirit within me.
Do not cast me away from your presence,
nor deprive me of your holy spirit.
For in sacrifice you take no delight,
burnt offering from me you would refuse,
my sacrifice, a contrite spirit.
A humbled, contrite heart you will not spurn.

(From Psalm 51)

Gospel: Matthew 9.9–13

Jesus antagonized the scribes who suspected him of false doctrine; he antagonized the Pharisees who objected to his associating with people who were unclean; he aroused complaint even from the followers of John the Baptist who thought he was not ascetic enough.

The incident recorded in today's Gospel reading reports how when he went to dinner – possibly a party – at the house of a tax-collector, the Pharisees asked his disciples why Jesus was so ready to consort with tax-collectors and sinners. By addressing their question to the disciples, they showed that they were reluctant even to speak with Jesus.

The tax-collectors worked for the Roman government and many of them feathered their own nests in the process, and so were hated both for their swindling and for their collaboration with the enemy. By 'sinners' were denoted all people who, although Jews by race and religion, were non-practising. They could be likened to the lapsed Christians of today.

By associating with these people Jesus did not intend to approve of their behaviour; he simply showed that the wish of their heavenly Father was that they should repent and enjoy the fullness of life he wanted them to enjoy; and so he was happy to join them in one of their parties.

Our Lord's remark, 'It is not the healthy who need the doctor, but the sick', contains hidden irony – sarcasm perhaps. Those who consider themselves righteous may not be so righteous after all; perhaps they have a certain spiritual kinship with the very people they despise.

St Catherine of Siena said that when she saw a sin in someone she was moved to confess – 'that is my fault', meaning not that she had caused their sin, but that she detected the same sin in herself – at least in its beginnings.

Sunday 11(A)

Old Testament thought:
I carried you on eagles' wings and brought you to myself.
(Exodus 19.4)

Vocal prayer:
Serve the Lord with gladness.
Come before him, singing for joy.
    We are his people, the sheep of his flock.
Know that he, the Lord, is God.
He made us, we belong to him.
Indeed, how good is the Lord,
eternal his merciful love.
He is faithful from age to age.
    We are his people, the sheep to his flock.

(From Psalm 100)

Gospel: Matthew 9.36–10.8

At all times Jesus was motivated by one impulse: compassion for the human race – a compassion which reflected the compassion of his heavenly Father, and was born of his perfect love for his Father. The biblical image of hungry sheep without a shepherd applied first of all to the people of Israel, but it is equally applicable to all of mankind. All men and women are hungry for the bread of life that is the Word of God.

Jesus was and is that Word of the Father, the Truth that has become accessible to us in the human words of Jesus our Lord. His compassion was shown in his effort to speak that Word to us, and to ensure its continued proclamation through the ministry of his apostles. And so he sent out the Twelve on a practice-run to their own people. The signs that were to accompany their preaching were those the prophets had said would herald the inauguration of the kingdom of God.

In this incident Jesus used another image – that of harvest, which has overtones of judgement. The coming of the kingdom is a time of judgement; and men and women will be judged by their reaction to the Gospel preached by the apostles. Will they be gathered with the wheat or with the chaff?

On this occasion Jesus instructed the Twelve to go only to their own people. That ancient people of God were to be privileged to be the first to hear the gospel of new covenant.

Sunday 12(A)

Old Testament thought:
I have committed my cause to you.
Sing to the Lord,
for he has delivered the soul of the needy
from the hands of evil men.   (Jeremiah 20.13)

Vocal prayer:
I burn with zeal for your house
and taunts against you fall on me.
In your great love, answer me, O God,
with your help that never fails:
Lord, answer, for your love is kind;
in your compassion turn towards me.
The Lord listens to the needy
and does not spurn his servants in their chains.
Let the heavens and the earth give him praise,
the sea and all its living creatures.   (From Psalm 69)

Gospel: Matthew 10.26–33

The reading from the prophet Jeremiah introduces the theme of today's Gospel. Jeremiah had spoken the word of God to his contemporaries: they disliked what he said and turned against him, threatening his life. All of the Old Testament prophets were treated in much the same way. The word of God was unpopular, because it judged the evil deeds of men and women. It is still unpopular.

Our Lord warned his disciples – especially the Twelve – that they too would arouse dislike, even hatred, from those to whom they proclaimed the gospel. In the face of persecution and ridicule – one of the hardest forms of persecution to resist – Christians in every generation will be tempted to deny their faith. To use Jeremiah's terminology, they may be 'seduced into error'. It is necessary therefore for Christians to strengthen themselves in advance against this temptation, for to succumb to it would be to risk rejection by our Lord on the day of judgement.

Denial of the faith can be either by rejection of the fundamental facts of the death and resurrection of our Lord, or by departure from the very strict moral demands that our Lord makes upon us.

SUNDAYS IN ORDINARY TIME, CYCLE B

Sunday 2(B)

Old Testament thought:
Each morning he wakes me to hear,
to listen like a disciple.
The Lord God has opened my ear.   (Isaiah 50.4–5)

Vocal prayer:
I waited, I waited for the Lord

and he stooped down to me;

he heard my cry.

He put a new song into my mouth,

a song of praise to our God.

In the scroll of the book it stands written

that I should do your will.

My God, I delight in your law

in the depth of my heart.   (From Psalm 40)

Gospel: John 1.35–42

The first few days of our Lord's public ministry are recorded by St John. John the Baptist told the religious leaders of the Jews that he was not himself the Messiah, but that one who was infinitely superior to him was already amongst them. The day after being interrogated by the religious leaders John the Baptist pointed Jesus out to the crowd as the Lamb of God that takes away the sins of the world, the one who had power to baptize with the Holy Spirit. The following day he pointed out Jesus as the Lamb of God to two of his own disciples. As he spoke he 'stared hard' at Jesus, indicating that this was no tentative opinion but an expression of inspired conviction.

John's two disciples left him and followed Jesus. They asked where he lived, went with him to his lodgings, and stayed all day. They became convinced that Jesus was the Messiah, and we can be sure that they asked him many questions and listened very carefully to all he had to say.

Next morning Andrew went straight off to tell his brother Simon that they had found the Messiah. Andrew brought Simon to Jesus who 'looked hard at him' and named him 'Peter' meaning 'Rock'. At the first moment of his public activity, Jesus laid the foundation of reliable testimony to his life and teaching in the person of Simon Peter and his successors.

The writer of this Gospel names only one of the two disciples who left John to follow Jesus; but he mentions the time of day when they did so. There is a strong hint here that the writer – St John – was an eyewitness of this event. Probably St John the Evangelist himself was the second of these two disciples.

Sunday 3(B)

Old Testament thought:
'Up!' the Lord said. 'Go to Nineveh, the great city, and preach to them as I bid you.'   (Jonah 3:2)

Vocal prayer:
Lord, make me know your ways.

Lord, teach me your paths.

Make me walk in your truth, and teach me:

for you are God my saviour.

Remember your mercy, Lord,

and the love you have shown from of old.

In your love remember me,

because of your goodness, O Lord.

The Lord is good and upright.

He shows the path to those who stray.

He guides the humble in the right path;

he teaches his way to the poor.   (From Psalm 25)

Gospel: Mark 1.14–20

The Father has acknowleged Jesus as his beloved Son, who has dedicated himself to the overthrow of evil. Jesus now begins to preach the Good News, but the shadow of the cross falls upon the scene: John has been arrested and will be beheaded; his fate foreshadows that of Jesus, who prudently moves off into Galilee, away from the hostile Jewish authorities.

Jesus first proclaims that the kingdom or, better, the 'kingly rule' of God is at hand. Salvation comes when a person falls under that kingly rule through repentance and faith in the power of Jesus. With the coming in flesh of the Son of God, and by his death and resurrection, the kingly rule of God has been established. Increase of that kingly rule in people's hearts in this world is effected by prayer and the sacraments, but that rule will be fully manifest only at the end of time.

The reading concludes with the call of the first four disciples. These men are to become fishers of men. Their apostleship lies in the future; for the time being they are to be disciples. The essence of their discipleship lies in cutting off from their past life, but the key factor in the incident is the authoritative person of Jesus. His call is the operative agent, not any merit in the ones called. Like them we, today's disciples, must realize that we did not choose him: he chose us.

Sunday 4(B)

Old Testament thought:

Moses said:
'Your God will raise up for you a prophet like myself,
from your own brothers; to him you must listen.'

(Deuteronomy 18:15)

Vocal prayer:

O that today you would listen to his voice!

Come, ring out our joy to the Lord;

hail the rock who saves us.

Let us come before him, giving thanks,

with songs let us hail the Lord.

Come in, let us kneel and bend low;

let us kneel before the God who made us

for he is our God and we

the people who belong to his pasture,

the flock that is led by his hand.

O that today you would listen to his voice!

Gospel: Mark 1.21–8

'God said "Let there be light", and there was light.' God's word is creative, his word is his act. After the divine epiphany at Mount Sinai men and women were afraid to confront God directly, and God promised that henceforth he would speak to them through human beings like Moses. And so down the ages God spoke to his chosen people through the prophets.

The prophets proclaimed who God was, what he intended to do, and called the people to respond in the way that God desired. The word was always related to action. In later Judaism the word of God spoken with power through a human voice became associated with the prophet of prophets, the Messiah, whose word would have power to judge, to forgive and to create new life in God's people.

In today's Gospel reading we meet the Messiah who on his first appearance in a synagogue demonstrated the divine power of the Word. His words are not recorded, but we are told that his audience sensed the power, the authority with which he spoke. They were touched deeply in their hearts and consciences. Their response may have been hesitant, but that of the demons was not. An evil spirit that was tormenting one man loudly proclaimed who Jesus was: the Anointed of God, who had come to destroy all that is evil. The word of Jesus drove out the demon.

At the beginning of his Gospel Mark had announced his theme: the duel between the Son of God and the Prince of Darkness; thus our Lord's first miracle was an exorcism, and his words, having an immediate effect, recall the opening words of the Bible: 'God said, and it was so'.

Sunday 5(B)

Old Testament thought:
Lying in bed I wonder, 'When will it be day?'
Risen I think, 'How slowly evening comes!'   (Job 7.4)

Vocal prayer:
Praise the Lord who heals the broken-hearted.
Praise the Lord for he is good;
sing to our God for he is loving:
to him our praise is due.
The Lord builds up Jerusalem
and brings back Israel's exiles,
he heals the broken-hearted,
he binds up all their wounds.
Our Lord is great and almighty;
his wisdom can never be measured.
The Lord raises the lowly;
he humbles the wicked to the dust.
Praise the Lord who heals the broken-hearted.
                                        (From Psalm 147)

Gospel: Mark 1.29–39

Peter's mother-in-law is the first woman mentioned in Mark's Gospel. When healed, her first act was to serve Jesus. In this we see a model of discipleship.

Throughout his Gospel Mark portrays the healing power of Jesus as the defeat of the malice of the Devil, whose ultimate desire is to drive men and women to despair. The demons, being pure spirits, have no difficulty in recognizing who Jesus is, and they fear him as their arch-enemy.

A central feature in this passage is our Lord's demonstration of how he, the eternal Son of God for ever in union with the Father, was obliged, because he had assumed a human nature, to realize in a human fashion constant and perfect union with God the Father, and to dedicate himself to the Father's service through regular times of solitary prayer. Only in this way could he gain and sustain the strength to serve mankind. He also set us an example which we must follow if we are to become disciples. Every one of us needs to spend some time each day in solitary prayer if we are to grow in grace and apostolic effectiveness.

The introduction to this Sunday's liturgy, provided in a popular edition of the German Sunday Missal, contains this wise comment. 'Life makes great demands on us all, and we often say that we have no time. Very true – we have no time to lose. But is that time lost in which we return ever and again to the source from which we live?'

Sunday 6(B)

Old Testament thought:
As long as the disease lasts he must live apart; he must live
outside the camp.

(Leviticus 13.46)

Vocal prayer:
Happy the man whose offence is forgiven,
whose sin is remitted.
O happy the man to whom the Lord
imputes no guilt,
in whose spirit is no guile.
But now I have acknowledged my sins;
my guilt I did not hide.
I said, 'I will confess
my offence to the Lord.'
And you, Lord, have forgiven
the guilt of my sin.
O come, ring out your joy,
all you upright of heart.   (From Psalm 32)

Gospel: Mark 1.40–5

The Jewish law did not prescribe any cure for leprosy; it merely protected others against it by excluding the one with the disease from all human contact. Our Lord's ability to cure a leper was an implicit declaration that he could do what the Law could not. 'God has done what the Law, weakened by the flesh, could not do: sending his own Son in the likeness of sinful flesh and as a sin offering he condemned sin in the flesh' (Romans 8.3).

St Paul had in mind spiritual sickness, but in the Jewish mind sickness was the work of the evil one, and so a symbol of sin. Leprosy, because of the way it pervaded the body, was in a class by itself, and in the New Testament cure of leprosy is always described as 'cleansing' not 'healing'. The person had to be cleansed from the spirit of evil which was the root cause of the illness. The root of all actual sin lies in the spiritual debility resulting from original sin, and so the cleansing of the leper can be seen as a sign of the cleansing from original sin through the sacrament of baptism.

Having touched the leper – a sign that he had no fear of the evil spirit – Jesus drove the spirit away. The man was then commanded to keep quiet about the miracle, and to report to the priest and carry out the purification rituals prescribed by the law. After that he could rejoin the worshipping community, just as men and women who have been cleansed from the root cause of sin through baptism, or from the stain of actual sins through the sacrament of reconciliation, may return to worship God in communion with his holy people.

Sunday 7(B)

Old Testament thought:
See, I am doing a new deed,
even now it comes to light; can you not see it?

(Isaiah 43.19)

Vocal prayer:
Happy the man who considers the poor and the weak.
The Lord will save him in the day of evil,
will guard him, give him life, make him happy in the land
and will not give him up to the will of his foes.
The Lord will help him on his bed of pain,
he will bring him back from sickness to health.
As for me, I said: 'Lord, have mercy on me,
heal my soul for I have sinned against you.'

(From Psalm 41)

Gospel: Mark 2.1–12

The paralytic and his kind friends hoped, quite simply, for a miracle of healing; but before Jesus gave the command: 'Pick up your stretcher and go off home', he said: 'My child, your sins are forgiven'. By giving forgiveness of sins priority over healing of the body, Jesus emphasized the fact that the mission of the Son of Man was to take away the sins of the world.

This action of Jesus brought him into immediate conflict with the scribes who were present. They accused him of blasphemy, for only God can forgive sins. Jesus would have agreed with them that no man has the right to forgive sins. He was asserting, therefore, that he was no mere man: he was 'the Son of Man', the Anointed of God, and his mission was to forgive, for he was one with the Father. This miracle of healing the paralytic is especially important, because it was designed as a proclamation by Jesus himself of who he really is.

The Jews hoped for forgiveness at the end of time, when the Messianic kingdom had been inaugurated. Jesus affirmed by this miracle, and by his frequent acts of forgiveness, that this kingdom had now come. Forgiveness could be obtained by men and women here and now. The Church is the embryonic kingdom of God upon earth, and that is why the ministry of forgiveness in the name of Christ is the foundation of the Church's mission.

Sunday 8(B)

Old Testament thought:
I will betroth you to myself with faithfulness,
and you will come to know the Lord.   (Hosea 2.22)

Vocal prayer:
My soul give thanks to the Lord,
all my being, bless his holy name.
My soul give thanks to the Lord
and never forget all his blessings.
The Lord is compassion and love,
slow to anger and rich in mercy.
He does not treat us according to our sins
nor repay us according to our faults.
As far as the east is from the west
so far does he remove our sins.
As a father has compassion on his sons,
the Lord has pity on those who fear him.

(From Psalm 103)

Gospel: Mark 2.18–22

The main statement in this passage is that the Messianic Age has come: the Bridegroom is here; therefore it is a time for joy and not for sorrow (fasting). Those who were still sorrowing – the disciples of John the Baptist – had not fully understood that the Messianic Age had come.

The parables of the old garment and the old wineskins illustrates this contrast. The wine of the Messianic kingdom cannot be contained within the wineskin of Judaism. The kingdom of the Messiah is not like pieces added to the old, but is a new driving force which bursts out of the straitjacket of the old Covenant, as young, still-fermenting wine bursts out of an old, brittle wineskin.

This statement, with its illustrative parables, is comparable with the saying that the least in the kingdom of heaven is greater than John the Baptist, and also with St Paul's teaching about the superiority of the spirit of Christianity over the spirit of Judaism.

Our Lord's affirmation on this occasion implies too that he, the Messiah, is on a par with Yahweh (the Lord God) for it was Yahweh and not the Messiah whom the Old Testament had presented as the husband of his people.

The equation of fasting with sorrow gives us a hint of how we ought to regard fasting. Fasting is not valuable in itself. Its object is to free us from distractions so that we may contemplate our Lord. The desolation of the disciples on Good Friday shows us what fasting really is. On that day would they have felt like eating? Can we by fasting share their experience?

Sunday 9(B)

Old Testament thought:
'You were a servant in the land of Egypt,
and the Lord your God brought you out from there.'
(Deuteronomy 5.15)

Vocal prayer:
Ring out your joy to God our strength.
Raise a song and sound the timbrel,
the sweet-sounding harp and the lute,
blow the trumpet at the new moon,
when the moon is full, on our feast.
Ring out your joy to God our strength.
A voice I did not know said to me:
'I freed your shoulder from the burden;
yours hands were freed from the load.
You called in distress and I saved you.'
Ring out your joy to God our strength.
(From Psalm 81)

Gospel: Mark 2.23–3.6

The incident recorded in the Gospel for today raises the question of the meaning of the Sabbath. Originally the Sabbath was to be quite simply a day of complete rest, symbolizing the relief of the Israelites on their deliverance from Egypt. In the course of time the Pharisees hedged this simple law about with innumerable prescriptions which purported to safeguard the law, but which only obscured its meaning, and frustrated its purpose, for it is much easier to hold to the letter of fussy little regulations than to fulfil the spiritual demands of God's genuine law.

The response to the Psalm in today's liturgy sets the tone of the true Sabbath: 'Ring out your joy to God our strength'. The keynote of the Sabbath is joy. The memory of the liberation from Egypt was the background to this law. In most of the nations in the Near East there were two distinct classes, the despotic rulers who lived in luxurious idleness, and the rest who lived in unremitting toil. In response to God's having freed them from slavery, the Israelites were obliged to grant to every person in their society a day of complete rest. It was to be a day when their sole activity was to realize their humanity – to worship God and enjoy one another's company.

For us who have even more to be thankful for than the Israelites had, the day when we commemorate our Lord's rising from the dead is a day of supreme joy when, setting aside all worry about working and making money, we lay hold of the great gift of freedom which allows us to worship God and rejoice with our families and friends in the good life God has given us.

Sunday 10(B)

Old Testament thought:
'I will make you enemies of each other:
you and the woman,
your offspring and her offspring.
It will crush your head
and you will strike its heel.'   (Genesis 3.15)

Vocal prayer:
If you, O Lord, should mark our guilt,
Lord, who would survive?
But with you is found forgiveness:
for this we revere you.
My soul is waiting for the Lord,
I count on his word.
My soul is longing for the Lord
more than watchman for daybreak.
Because with the Lord there is mercy
and fullness of redemption,
Israel indeed he will redeem
from all its iniquity.   (From Psalm 130)

Gospel: Mark 3.20–35

In bringing men and women into his kingdom through the gateway of forgiveness, Jesus had less difficulty with sinners than with the leaders of the religious establishment, and even with some of his blood relations. This theme features prominently in St John's Gospel, where it is announced in the Prologue: 'He came to his own and his own received him not'. This is the theme dealt with in today's reading from St Mark's Gospel.

The Jersusalem scribes closed their eyes to the love that Jesus showed as he expelled demons from men and women. They went so far as to assert that he did this by the power of the very one he was casting out. Jesus rebutted this assertion, pointing out that if it were true, then Satan's kingdom was disintegrating. No, he was the stronger man who was able to burgle the house of the strong man within – in this case, Satan.

Jesus went farther than a mere refutation of the scribes' accusation. He accused them of committing a sin against the Holy Spirit, by persisting in calling light darkness, shutting their eyes to his love, and thus disqualifying themselves for forgiveness. He was not teaching that there is a particular sin that is unforgivable, but that persistence in the refusal to acknowledge him and to repent, prevents his forgiveness becoming effective.

The Gospel reading ends with Jesus' statement that all who believe in his word, and do his will are his genuine relations.

Sunday 11(B)

Old Testament thought:
I will plant the cedar myself on the high mountain.
It will sprout branches and bear fruit,
and become a noble cedar.
Every kind of bird will live beneath it,
every winged creature rest in the shade of its branches.

(Ezekiel 17.23)

Vocal prayer:
It is good to give thanks to the Lord,
to play in honour of your name, O Most High,
to proclaim your love at daybreak
and your faithfulness all through the night
to the music of the zither and lyre,
to the rippling of the harp.
The virtuous flourish like palm trees
and grow as tall as the cedars of Lebanon.
Planted in the house of the Lord,
they will flourish in the courts of our God,
still bearing fruit in old age,
still remaining fresh and green.   (From Psalm 92)

Gospel: Mark 4.26–34

In the first parable the sower is God and we are the seed he sows in his field. The field is God's creation and supports the mystery of growth. Natural growth is a mystery; even more mysterious is growth in grace. At exactly the right time the owner of the field harvests the crop. The accent in this parable is on the maturing of the separate plants, so that the kingdom of God is being likened to the control God exercises over the spiritual maturing of each individual person, until he is fit to be gathered into the heavenly barn.

The accent in the second parable is on the corporate life of Christians, that is on the Church. Out of a very small seed grows up a mighty bush that gives shelter to countless birds. This parable exhorts the Church – that is us – to fulfil its function, world-wide and locally, of becoming a home for all people, the great shelter wherein all people can find the light of Truth and the nourishment of the sacraments.

Sunday 12(B)

Old Testament thought:
Who pent up the sea behind closed doors
when it leapt tumultuous out of the womb?   (Job 38.8)

Vocal prayer:
To you have I lifted up my eyes,
you who dwell in the heavens:
my eyes, like the eyes of slaves
on the hand of their lords.
Like the eyes of a servant
on the hand of her mistress,
so our eyes are on the Lord our God
till he show us his mercy.
Have mercy on us, Lord, have mercy.
We are filled with contempt.
Indeed all too full is our soul
with the scorn of the rich,
with the proud man's disdain.   (Psalm 123)

Gospel: Mark 4:35–41

Preparing his disciples for their future mission, Jesus taught them first in a series of parables (Mark 4.1–34); then in a series of miracles (Mark 4.35–5.43), which may be regarded as action-parables, for belief in the miracles of Jesus consists not simply in believing that they happened, but in grasping their meaning.

The miracle read today contains three scenes: 1. the storm-tossed boat is contrasted with the tranquil sleep of Jesus; 2. the terror of the professional fishermen is contrasted with the sovereign calm of the Master who commands the waves with authority; 3. the awe-stricken reaction of the disciples to this display of cosmic power.

In the Old Testament, control over the sea is a characteristic sign of divine power (Job 7.12; Psalms 74.13; 89.8–9; 93.3–4; Isaiah 51.9–10); peaceful sleep is a sign of perfect trust in God (Proverbs 3.23–4; Psalms 3.5; 4.8; Job 11.18–19). This is the clue to understanding the catechetical purpose of the incident. Jesus, by his behaviour, reproaches the Twelve for their lack of trust in God, then by calming the storm he evokes the question: 'Who is this?' As yet they had not discovered who their Master really was, hence their lack of faith. It was now beginning to dawn on them that he was one with the Lord of heaven and earth, who alone can command the elements.

Sundays in Ordinary Time, Cycle C

Sunday 2(C)

Old Testament thought:
As the bridegroom rejoices in his bride,
so will your God rejoice in you.   (Isaiah 62.5)

Vocal prayer:
O sing a new song to the Lord,

sing to the Lord all the earth.

O sing to the Lord, bless his name.

Give the Lord, you families of peoples,

give the Lord glory and power,

give the Lord the glory of his name.

Worship the Lord in his temple.

O earth, tremble before him.

Proclaim to the nations: 'God is king.'

He will judge the peoples in fairness.   (From Psalm 96)

Gospel: John 2.1–12

Three episodes in the Gospel story: the adoration of the Magi, the Baptism of our Lord in the Jordan, and the miracle-sign of changing water into wine at the wedding-feast in Cana are linked together as aspects of the Epiphany. In each of these events the glory of Jesus is revealed.

At the wedding in Cana Jesus at first hesitates, explaining to his mother that his 'hour' has not come, that is to say, his full glory cannot be seen until the hour of his passion, death, and resurrection. None the less he agrees to 'let his glory be seen', that is, to give a glimpse of that glory through a sign. This first miracle announces that his subsequent miracles too must be seen as signs of his glory. The connection between this first sign and the hour of his glory is hinted at by St John who tells us that the event took place 'after three days' – an allusion to the three days of waiting for the Resurrection.

The sign is a commentary on St John the Baptist's affirmation that he, John, baptized with water, whereas the one who was to come, the Messiah, would baptize with the Holy Spirit and fire. John's baptism is to Jesus' baptism as water is to wine. The ritual purifications of the Jews, suggested by the water-jars, was about to be replaced by the real purification effected by the Holy Spirit of Christ.

At this first manifestation of her Son's glory Mary, in the name of us all, pleaded with her Son to bestow his gift of life upon us. She appears again, according to St John, only at the 'Hour' of his glory on the cross, when her Son commended her as mother to John, representative of all her children.

Sunday 3(C)

Old Testament thought:
Ezra the scribe stood on a wooden dais; Ezra read from
the Law of God, translating and giving the sense, so that
the people understood.   (From Nehemiah 8.4–8)

Vocal prayer:
The law of the Lord is perfect,

it revives the soul.

The rule of the Lord is to be trusted,

it gives wisdom to the simple.

The precepts of the law are right,

they gladden the heart.

The command of the Lord is clear,

it gives light to the eyes.

The fear of the Lord is holy,

abiding for ever.

The decrees of the Lord are truth

and all of them just.   (From Psalm 19)

Gospel: Luke 1.1–4; 4.14–21

The Gospel passage today contains the first few verses of St Luke's Gospel, in which he states his purpose and method in writing. The basic facts of the Faith, he admits, were already known and believed by many, for the apostles had been preaching for several years. Luke tells us that his object is, by collecting evidence from eyewitnesses – that is from the apostles and others who had been privileged with first-hand knowledge of the life and teaching of Jesus – to confirm the truth of what people had already heard. These few lines by St Luke help us to understand the relationship between the living voice and living tradition of the Church and the words of Scripture.

Our excerpt for today then moves on to the fourth chapter. Here we find Jesus, shortly after his baptism, in the synagogue of his home town at Nazareth. His travelling into Galilee was itself a fulfilment of the prophecy that light would one day return to that region, where it had been extinguished in 721 BC when the Assyrians took the people into captivity.

In the synagogue Jesus read out the prophecy of Isaiah about the anointed Servant of the Lord who was to come to proclaim salvation, to free captives, to open the eyes of the blind, and to liberate the oppressed. Then he affirmed that he was this Messiah, the Anointed One of God. There was a tense silence and all hung upon his words.

Sunday 4(C)

Old Testament thought:
Stand up and tell them all I command you.

(Jeremiah 1.17)

Vocal prayer:
In you, O Lord, I take refuge;
let me never be put to shame.
In your justice rescue me, free me:
pay heed to me and save me.
Be a rock where I can take refuge,
a mighty stronghold to save me;
for you are my rock, my stronghold.
Free me from the hand of the wicked.
My lips will tell of your justice
and day by day of your help.
O God, you have taught me from my youth
and I proclaim your wonders still.   (From Psalm 71)

Gospel: Luke 4.21–30

The prophecy that the Holy One of God would come to earth had been fulfilled. Jesus of Nazareth stood there amongst his own kith and kin in the synagogue of his home town and told the congregation that the prophecy had been fulfilled, and so doing proclaimed that he was that Holy One, the Messiah, God's Anointed.

At first the people of Nazareth were delighted. They smiled and said: 'Here at last is the Messiah, and he's one of us!' Jesus knew that this reaction was one of self-congratulation and selfish expectation. His reputation had gone before him in the province, and the people of Nazareth looked forward to his providing health, prosperity, and political power for the nation, in which they would surely occupy a privileged position.

Jesus burst the bubble of their pride, telling them that 'no prophet is ever accepted in his own country', and that in times past it had been a Sidonian woman who showed hospitality to the prophet Elijah, and a Syrian soldier who, through faith in the word of a prophet, had been cured of leprosy. The notion that gentiles could be preferred to themselves, members of the chosen race, infuriated the congregation in the synagogue, so that they attempted to kill Jesus, but he 'walked away' – as he does from all who reject him.

Jesus might well have been killed on that occasion, but he escaped mysteriously, for his 'hour' had not yet come. The incident was, however, a foreshadowing of the hatred, born of national and religious pride, that would eventually bring about his death.

Sunday 5(C)

Old Testament thought:
I saw the Lord seated on a high throne;
his train filled the sanctuary;
I said: 'What a wretched state I am in! I am lost,
for I am a man of unclean lips
and I live among a people of unclean lips,
and my eyes have looked at the King, the Lord of hosts.'

(From Isaiah 6)

Vocal prayer:
Before the angels I will bless you, O Lord.
I thank you Lord, with all my heart,
you have heard the words of my mouth.
Before the angels I will bless you.
I will adore before your holy temple.   (From Psalm 138)

Gospel: Luke 5.1–11

First we note the similarity between the account of Isaiah's vision of God above the holy of holies in the temple and his being called to take God's word to the people, and the Gospel story of Simon Peter's confrontation with the Son of God on the lakeside. Both men were overawed by the divine holiness and became acutely aware of their sinfulness; both were reassured and granted forgiveness and purification, and in addition were offered a commission to work for God.

Next we note the contrast between the incident in today's Gospel and that in last week's Gospel. The congregation in the synagogue at Nazareth had recognized our Lord's divine power, for they knew he had worked miracles elsewhere, but instead of bowing down before him in contrition and supplication, they rejected him because they could see that he was not going to serve their pride and worldly ambition.

One scene warns us against perverse notions of what Christ's kingship means: the other two describe what true discipleship entails. Isaiah's and Simon Peter's reactions typify the spiritual disposition that must be found not just in the leaders of the Church, but in every believer, whose Christian life begins in adoration of Christ the Lord, joined with humble confession of unworthiness, followed by the acceptance of forgiveness and readiness to serve God.

Sunday 6(C)

Old Testament thought:
A blessing on the man who puts his trust in the Lord,
with the Lord for his hope.   (Jeremiah 17.7)

Vocal prayer:
As a doe longs for running streams,

so my soul longs for you, my God.

My soul thirsts for God, the God of life;

when shall I go to see the face of God?

I have no food but tears, day and night;

and all day long men say to me: 'Where is your God?'

I remember, and my soul melts within me:

I am on the way to the wonderful tent, to the house of
  God.

When my soul is downcast within me, I think of you;

from the land of Jordan and of Hermon, of you, humble
  mount Zion.

Why so downcast my soul, why do you sigh within me?

Put your hope in God: I shall praise him yet, my saviour,
  my God.   (From Psalm 42)

Gospel: Luke 6.17, 20–6

After praying the whole night long on the mountain, Jesus chose twelve from the larger crowd of disciples. The number indicated that these men and their successors, whom they in turn would appoint, stood in relation to the Church as the twelve patriarchs stood to Israel. Through Abraham's posterity the transmission of God's blessing had been promised to the whole world: through the Twelve apostles, the realization of that blessing would at last be accomplished. And so when Jesus came down from his prayer on the mountain the Twelve came with him, surrounding him as he addressed first those who had already begun to believe in him, that is the disciples, and then the uncommitted crowd on the fringe.

The words that Jesus spoke on this occasion are known as the 'Beatitudes'. They are not a systematized moral–theological code, answering specific moral problems, but a description of 'the general stance and attitudes which underlie all Christian life and behaviour' (Eugène LaVerdiere SSS). Nor in the Beatitudes is Jesus contrasting believers with unbelievers, for the woes, too, are directed at disciples, but he is pointing out that not all believers will act as he has commanded.

The blessed are those who place no reliance on worldly help, but have perfect trust in God alone; and this disposition is their blessing; but for those who aggressively put their trust and hope in worldly power and pleasure, and are capable of laughing at the sufferings of others, punishment is waiting.

Sunday 7(C)

Old Testament thought:
The godless is for ever coveting,
the virtuous man gives without ever refusing.

(Proverbs 21.26)

Vocal prayer:
My soul, give thanks to the Lord,
all my being, bless his holy name.
My soul, give thanks to the Lord
and never forget all his blessings.
It is he who forgives all your guilt,
who heals every one of your ills,
who redeems your life from the grave,
who crowns you with love and compassion.
The Lord is compassion and love,
slow to anger and rich in mercy,
he does not treat us according to our sins
nor repay us according to our faults.   (From Psalm 103)

Gospel: Luke 6.27–38

Having taught his disciples about the interior stance that ought to characterize those within the kingdom, that is the Church, Jesus goes on to develop the ethics of the kingdom, addressing now the wider group of those who were listening, although what is said applies to disciples also. But Jesus is now addressing all mankind, for all are potential disciples.

The content of his teaching is not complicated; it deals with the way we treat one another; it is a concrete application of the attitude embodied in the Beatitudes. In this passage the themes are 1. *love of enemies* and 2. *generosity in giving*.

1. The slap on the cheek is an insult, not an assault, and so the saying of Jesus is not about the ethics of self-defence but about the way we react to insult. We must not be over-sensitive about our own importance and spring to return insult with insult, for that is to offend the dignity of another human being. In the story of David (the first Old Testament reading) David refrained from taking revenge because Saul was the Lord's Anointed. Every human being is anointed with the image of God, and so we must never treat another with contempt, even if he has so treated us.

2. The worldly person tends to give with an eye to getting something in return. Those within the kingdom of God must give with absolutely no ulterior motive. Such selfless generosity will be seen chiefly in giving to the very poor, these who are so poor that they are reduced to begging or even to stealing. The true disciple ought to be sensitive to the plight of such people, and ready to help them even before any demand is made.

Sunday 8(C)

Old Testament thought:
The orchard where the tree grows is judged by the
  quality of its fruit,
similarly a man's words betray what he feels.

(Ecclesiasticus 27.6–7)

Vocal prayer:
God, create a clean heart in me,

put into me a new and constant spirit,

do not banish me from your presence,

do not deprive me of your holy spirit.

Be my saviour again, renew my joy,

keep my spirit ready and willing;

and I shall teach transgressors the way to you,

and to you the sinner will return

Save me from death, God my saviour,

and my tongue will acclaim your righteousness;

Lord, open my lips,

and my mouth will speak out your praise.

(From Psalm 51)

Gospel: Luke 6.39–45

Jesus completed the train of thought he had begun with the Beatitudes by telling a series of parables. Consider first of all the sentence that follows the first parable: 'The fully-trained disciple will be like his teacher'.

The Twelve apostles are standing beside Jesus as he teaches the people on this occasion; they are, or are to become, the most perfectly-trained disciples and will be commissioned to teach in his name. They, above all people, must imitate their Master, especially in his humility; but all disciples in every age, represented by the group of disciples in the crowd before Jesus, are called to be instruments of handing on his gospel to others, represented in the crowd by the men and women from many regions who are standing around on the edge of the crowd. Their apostolic work as disciples, like that of the Twelve, will not be effective unless they too imitate the humility of Jesus.

We come to the parables. Before becoming vehicles of the light of Christ to others, we must ourselves become enlightened by faith in our Lord and his gospel. If we are blind, how can we lead others? The parable of the man with a plank in his eye trying to take a splinter out of another person's eye reinforces the first part of the parable, and suggests also that self-examination and repentance are prerequisites for effective evangelism.

The third parable, about sound and rotten trees in an orchard, invites us to recall the parable of the vine and the branches in St John's Gospel. We remain healthy branches only if we remain firmly engrafted on to the stock that is Christ. Our ability to enlighten others depends upon our being nourished ourselves from Christ through prayer and the sacraments. Our actions will flow form what we are – healthy, living branches growing up from the vine-stock.

Sunday 9(C)

Old Testament thought:
Solomon said: 'And the foreigner too, if he comes from a
　distant land
and prays in this Temple, hear from heaven where your
home is,
　and grant all the foreigner asks.'

(1 Kings 8.41–2)

Vocal prayer:
Praise the Lord, all you nations,
acclaim him all you peoples!
Strong is his love for us;
he is faithful for ever.

(Psalm 117)

Gospel: Luke 7.1–10

The exclusive and self-righteous mind of many of the Jewish leaders in our Lord's day was not by any means in harmony with the real mood of the Old Testament, but the bigoted contemporaries of our Lord demonstrate how even a true and pure religion can become debased.

The Gospel passage read on this Sunday is introduced and matched by a passage from the first book of Kings which reports Solomon's prayer for the gentiles. In the prophets too we find the Israelites being exhorted to open their hearts and minds to the nations, and to rejoice at the thought of their coming to worship the one true God in the Temple at Jersusalem.

When Jesus showed how ready he was to go down to Capernaum and heal the slave of a Roman centurion, he was following the best tradition of his people. And we note that it was the elders of the synagogue at Capernaum who came at the centurion's request, and interceded with Jesus on his behalf.

They present their request in Jewish terms, it is true, for they say: 'He deserves this of you, because he is friendly to our people; in fact, he is the one who built the synagogue'; but their intercession demonstrates that they were prepared to share the privileges of their faith with other nations. In his prayer, Solomon too had expressed the thought that the disposition of the non-Israelite was important, in the phrase: 'if he comes from a distant country *for the sake of your name'*.

The episode recorded by St Luke in this part of his Gospel is prophetic also. The elders of the synagogue are going to be replaced by the presbyters of the early Church (for whom Luke was writing his Gospel) and the centurion can be seen as an forerunner of the first fruits of the gentile converts who would be welcomed into the new Israel.

Sunday 10(C)

Old Testament thought:
Elijah cried out to the Lord,
'Lord my God, may the soul of this child, I beg you, come
   into him again!'
The Lord heard the prayer of Elijah, and the soul of the
   child returned.   (1 Kings 17.21–2)

Vocal prayer:
I will praise you, Lord, you have rescued me
and have not let my enemies rejoice over me.
O Lord, you have raised my soul from the dead,
restored me to life from those who sink into the grave.
Sing psalms to the Lord, you who love him,
give thanks to his holy name.
His anger lasts a moment; his favour all through life.
At night there are tears, but joy comes with dawn.
The Lord listened and had pity.
The Lord came to my help.
For me you have changed my mourning into dancing;
O Lord my God, I will thank you for ever.

                                              (From Psalm 30)

Gospel: Luke 7.11–17

One of the ways the Lord accredited his prophets in Old Testament times was by enabling them, through prayer, to work miracles. Elijah, for example, was accredited in this way. Our Lord, who is the prophet *par excellence*, was accredited in the same manner; but the miracles of our Lord contained a dimension that distinguished them from the miracles performed by the prophets. Jesus performed his miracles out of compassion for individuals, it is true, but they spoke of his much wider compassion for all mankind. His miracles were significant for his whole redemptive action.

We read today of his restoring to life of the son of the widow at Nain. The setting of this miracle was totally Jewish, whereas the setting of the healing of the slave, which is recorded in the immediately preceding text of Luke, was gentile. The raising of the widow's son was designed, therefore, to declare that the Jewish faith had to be resurrected so that its adherents might enter the new Israel, for in our Lord's day the religion of the Jews had become moribund.

Members of the new Israel today must be constantly on their guard lest they allow *their* faith to become moribund.

Sunday 11(C)

Old Testament thought:
David said to Nathan, 'I have sinned against the Lord.'
Nathan said to David, 'The Lord, for his part, forgives
  your sin;
you are not to die'.   (2 Samuel 12.13)

Vocal prayer:
Happy the man whose offence is forgiven,
whose sin is remitted.
O happy the man to whom the Lord
imputes no guilt,
in whose spirit is no guile.
But now I have acknowledged my sins;
my guilt I did not hide.
I said: 'I will confess
my offence to the Lord.'
And you, Lord, have forgiven
the guilt of my sin.
Rejoice, rejoice in the Lord,
exult, you just!
O come, ring out your joy,
all you upright of heart.   (From Psalm 32)

Gospel: Luke 7.36–8.3

The incident we examine today took place in the house of a Pharisee, a man who considered himself to be a representative of the pure Jewish faith. He had invited Jesus to a meal, and while at table Jesus was approached by a 'woman of the town' who burst into tears, bowed low in an act of worship, and anointed his feet both with her tears and with costly ointment. In this scene Luke wants to show the contrast between the Pharisee's attitude to the woman and the attitude of Jesus, and so throw light on what our Lord's forgiveness really is, and what disposition of heart and mind is required in the penitent who seeks forgiveness.

It has to be admitted that in the way Luke tells this story a question is left unresolved: is forgiveness given because love is shown to our Lord, or is love shown because forgiveness has been received? But we can set this problem aside, for the final message of the incident is that the woman – who represents all sinners – is moved by recognition of *who Jesus is*, that is by faith joined with love, and this faith moves her to ask, with tears, for forgiveness which the Lord gives immediately. He welcomes her into the peace of his kingdom. Her past life is gone.

For the Pharisee the dominant consideration was that the woman was degenerate, and even if she were pardoned for past offences she was still the same bad lot and would never be more than a second-class citizen in Israel.

Jesus made clear that in the new Israel there is no such ting as a second-class citizen. Every believing repentant sinner is welcomed in the 'Church in which everyone is a "first-born son" and a citizen of heaven' (Hebrews 12.23).

Sunday 12(C)

Old Testament thought:
The will look upon the one whom they pierced.

(Zechariah 12.10)

Vocal prayer:
O God, you are my God, for you I long;
for you my soul is thirsting.
My body pines for you
like a dry, weary land without water
So I gaze on you in the sanctuary
to see your strength and your glory.
For your love is better than life,
my lips will speak of your praise.
For you have been my help;
in the shadow of your wings I rejoice.
My soul clings to you;
your right hand holds me fast.   (From Psalm 63)

Gospel: Luke 9.18–24

Jesus set the disclosure of his identity to the disciples in the context of prayer. After praying in the presence of the Twelve he asked them: 'Who do the crowds say I am?' They told him, and then he put them on he spot: 'But who do you say I am?'

Peter answered that he was the long-awaited Messiah, the Anointed of God; Jesus accepted this declaration, for it was true, but he added that this Son of Man would have to suffer and die and then rise from the dead on the third day. His use of the phrase 'Son of Man' emphazised the human nature and vulnerability of the true Messiah.

Most of the people were expecting the Messiah to be a conquering hero, and the apostles more or less shared this concept, so that Jesus found it hard to convince them that the Messiah was also the Suffering Servant of the Lord, who had figured in the prophecies of Isaiah. The true Messiah would conquer Satan and usher in the kingdom of God through sacrifice and not through force of arms.

Finally Jesus admonished the Twelve never to cling fearfully to life but to be ready to live and act perfectly in accordance with his teaching, whatever the consequences. In so doing they would find liberation of soul; freed from seeking security in nervous, self-centred materialism, they would attain to confidence centred upon God.